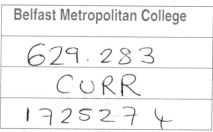

Driver's Handbook

Susan Curran

LONDON: THE STATIONERY OFFICE

Written and compiled by Susan Curran

Designed by Hannent©

Illustrations by Alan Batley

First published in 1997 by The Stationery Office Ltd.,
St Crispins, Duke Street, Norwich NR3 1PD

ISBN 0 11 702177 6

British Library Cataloguing in Publication Data

A CIP catalogue record for this book is available from
the British Library

Printed and bound in Great Britain by
Reflex Litho Limited, Thetford, Norfolk.

Foreword

If you've ever been unsure what your stopping distance is in the wet, worried over who you should tell when you buy a new car, or wondered whether you can refuse when a police officer asks you to take a breathalyser, then this book is for you.

We've tried to include all the information you'll need - plus some that's less essential, but that we hope you'll find interesting or entertaining. This is a book primarily for the general driver, rather than for the enthusiast or the professional. It's designed to sit in the glove compartment along with your car manual and map. Dip into it when you have a moment to kill, or check out the index when you need to know something in a hurry. When you need more in-depth information, the organisations listed in Section 11 should be able to assist you.

We've included as much detailed information as possible, but inevitably much of it is subject to change. The publishers cannot be responsible for any errors, and you are advised to check any essential details – for instance, speed limits and drink-driving limits for foreign countries – before acting upon them.

A book such as this draws information from many sources, and calls on the expertise of many individuals. Particular thanks is owing to the following:

Bill Smith OBE, former Chief Driving Examiner for England and Wales, kindly reviewed and commented on all of the text.

PC Peter Chapman of Norfolk Constabulary reviewed the sections relating to motoring offences.

Steve Hanley, consultant to the National Trailer & Towing Association, contributed information on towing regulations.

James Duffell of Norwich Union advised on insurance regulations.

Christine Nickles and her colleagues at the Driving Standards Agency provided information on driving test passes (and failures).

HMSO gave permission to quote from Crown Copyright sources (see page 6).

My thanks are due too to Samantha Bestwick, Rob Langley and Richard Nelson of The Stationery Office, and to Hannent© who designed the book and Alan Batley who drew the illustrations. We hope you'll find the result helpful and enjoyable to read.

Susan Curran
December 1997

Acknowledgments

The following Crown copyright material has been adapted with the permission of the Controller of Her Majesty's Stationery Office. The Controller accepts no responsibility for the context in which the material has been presented.

Hazchem symbols (page 18) reproduced from *The Highway Code* (Department of Transport).

Information on stopping distances (page 50) reproduced from *The Highway Code* (Department of Transport).

Information on speed limits (page 51) reproduced from *The Highway Code* (Department of Transport).

Information on seat belt requirements (page 53) reproduced from *The Highway Code* (Department of Transport).

Information on insurance claims (page 53) reproduced from *Road Accidents Great Britain 1996: The Casualty Report* (Department of the Environment, Transport and The Regions).

Information on the scope of the MOT test (pages 34 to 47) adapted from the *MOT Inspection Manual* (Vehicle Inspectorate).

Information on the relative ages of cars and owners (page 39) reproduced from *National Travel Survey 1993/95* (Department of Transport).

Information on why cars fail the MOT (page 41) reproduced from *Transport Statistics Great Britain 1997* (Department of the Environment, Transport and The Regions).

Information on the number of cars on the road (page 61) reproduced from *Transport Statistics Great Britain 1997* (Department of the Environment, Transport and The Regions).

Information on lengths of journeys (page 61) reproduced from *Road Traffic Statistics Great Britain 1995* (Department of Transport).

Information on bike and car journeys in Inner London (page 70) reproduced from *Journey Times Survey 1994, Inner and Outer London* (Department of Transport).

Information on car emissions (page 71) reproduced from *Transport Statistics Great Britain 1997* (Department of the Environment, Transport and The Regions).

Information on petrol prices (page 67) reproduced from *Transport Statistics Great Britain 1997* (Department of the Environment, Transport and The Regions).

Information on comparative national accident statistics (page 78) reproduced from *Transport Statistics Great Britain 1997* (Department of the Environment, Transport and The Regions).

Accident statistics (pages 82 and 84) reproduced from *Road Accidents Great Britain 1996: The Casualty Report* (Department of the Environment, Transport and The Regions).

Information on cars breaking the speed limit (page 83) reproduced from *Road Traffic Statistics Great Britain 1995* (Department of Transport).

Information on accident rates for different models of cars (page 82) reproduced from *Cars: Make and Model: The Risk of Driver Injury and Car Accident Rates in Great Britain: 1994* (Department of Transport).

Information on motorists convicted of motor vehicle offences (page 94) reproduced from *Transport Statistics Great Britain 1997* (Department of the Environment, Transport and The Regions).

Contents

| Contents

In an emergency

If you break down on the road

If you're not on a motorway:

- Get your car off the road if possible, and park in a safe location.

- If you can't get your car off the road and it's in a dangerous position, or causing an obstruction, switch on your hazard warning lights. Ask your passengers to wait in a safe place. (A lone woman may feel safest remaining in the car with the doors locked.)

- Put/keep your sidelights on if visibility is at all poor.

- If you carry a red warning triangle, set it on the road at least 50 m (164 ft) behind your car and on the same side of the road.

- At night or in poor visibility, don't stand behind your vehicle or let anyone else do so. It could stop other drivers seeing your lights.

- If anything falls off your car on to the road, stop at the next safe place and retrieve it as soon as it's safe to do so.

If you break down on a motorway:

- If at all possible, pull on to the hard shoulder and stop as far to the left as possible.
  If possible, stop near an emergency telephone.

- Switch on your hazard warning lights and, if needed for visibility, your sidelights.

- Set your warning triangle farther back: about 150 m (492 ft), on the hard shoulder.

- Both you and your passengers should leave the car by the left-hand door(s). Passengers should wait in a safe place away from the carriageway and the hard shoulder. (The bank is ideal.) Leave any animals in the car, but not people unless they feel at risk. The hard shoulder is a dangerous place: up to one in eight motoring deaths occurs there.

- If you don't have enough warning of the breakdown to reach the hard shoulder, switch on your hazard lights. Leave the car only if you're confident you can get clear of the carriageway safely. If in doubt, stay in your car wearing your seat belt and wait for the emergency services. Phone them if you have a mobile. Don't try to put a warning triangle on the carriageway.

- Walk to the nearest emergency phone. The arrows on the posts at the back of the hard shoulder will show you which way to go. In no circumstances cross the carriageway, and keep as far from it as you can while walking. Tell the police your location, and warn them if you're a woman travelling alone.

- Don't try to do even simple repairs on the motorway (including the hard shoulder). It's too dangerous. If anything falls from your car, don't try to pick it up. Stop at the next emergency phone and call the emergency services.

If you have a disability and can't follow the advice above:

- Stay in your car with all the doors locked.

- Switch on the hazard lights.

- Display a Help pennant or if you have a car phone, contact the emergency services.

If you break down on a level crossing:

- Get everyone out of the car and clear of the crossing immediately.

- If there's a railway telephone, use it immediately to tell the signal operator. Follow the instructions you're given.

- If possible, and if there's time before a train arrives, move the car clear of the crossing. If the alarm sounds or the amber light comes on, abandon the car and get well clear of the crossing.

Mechanical disaster

Regular maintenance of your car will help to ensure that it doesn't suffer too many faults when you're on the road. But if you do have a sudden problem, it's helpful for even the most engine-shy driver to have some idea what's causing it – and whether it can easily be remedied. These are some of the more common possibilities. Of course, this is not an exhaustive list: there could be other reasons for any symptom.

The car won't start
- The battery could be flat. Short term solution: a push start or jump start. (Avoid push starts if you have a catalytic converter or an automatic.) Permanent solution: recharge or replace the battery.

- The car could be out of fuel. Check the fuel gauge and/or the tank.

- There could be damp in the electrical circuits. An anti-damp spray will help to prevent and cure this.

- The starter motor could be jammed. Try leaving the vehicle in gear, turning the ignition off, and rocking the car back and forwards.

- There could be a fault in the spark electrical system. Check the components or seek expert help.

- If you persist in turning over the starter motor without success, you may flood the engine or clog the circuits. Give the engine time to recover and try again.

The temperature gauge heads to the red zone, or a temperature warning light comes on

- The engine's overheating. To drive on could be disastrous. Stop immediately.

- The fan belt may have snapped, or the fuse blown in an electric fan. Make emergency repairs, replace the fuse, or call for expert help.

- The radiator hose may be leaking. Make emergency repairs or call for expert help.

- The cooling system may be leaking. Check the coolant level (but don't remove the radiator cap while the engine is hot). If it's too low, add additional coolant. Don't add cold coolant to a hot engine: let it cool down first. Find out the source of the leak as soon as possible.

- You may have low oil pressure. See below.

The low oil pressure warning light comes on (after the car has started)

- Low oil pressure could have a disastrous effect on the engine. Stop immediately.

- Have you checked the oil level recently? If so, you have an oil leak or blockage. (If not, you may simply need to add oil.) Smoke coming from your exhaust and a rough-sounding engine (or one losing power rapidly) are additional symptoms. Check the level using the dipstick. If it's low, short-term solution: add oil. Permanent solution: locate and repair the leak, with expert help if necessary. If the level is normal, there's a blockage: seek help as necessary.

The ignition warning light comes on (after the car has started)

- Your battery isn't recharging. Investigate immediately. Various failures could cause this, some of them serious.

The brake warning light comes on

- Stop immediately and investigate. The brake fluid level may be too low. You need to know the cause (and have it topped up) before driving on. Alternatively the brake pads may need changing. Check your car handbook: it may be safe to drive cautiously to a garage to have this done.

The car suddenly steers heavily or erratically

- You may have a puncture. Stop immediately and change the wheel. Don't drive on to the nearest garage, you could do irreparable damage to the wheel.

If you witness an accident

If you're directly involved in the accident, or if it's arguable that your vehicle or your driving was a factor in the accident even though you didn't collide with another vehicle, see also pages 14/15.

- If you didn't come to a halt as a result of the accident, pull up safely, at the side of the road or on the hard shoulder if on a motorway.

- The vehicles directly involved in the accident shouldn't be moved until all the formalities are dealt with and all casualties removed, unless they're causing danger or a serious hold-up to other traffic. If it's necessary to move them, first mark their position on the road (getting an independent witness to note what happened if possible).

- (Unless you're safely parked) switch on your hazard lights. If you have a warning triangle, set it up in the road 50 m (164 ft) behind the vehicles. On a motorway, increase this distance to 150 m (492 ft) and set the triangle on the hard shoulder. If you don't have a warning triangle, ask someone to flag down any traffic.

- Ask any uninjured people to move from the vehicles to a safe place. On a motorway, the bank at the roadside is best. Don't let them cross a motorway carriageway or stay on the hard shoulder or central reservation.

- If the accident involved a vehicle carrying dangerous goods, you and your passengers should put out any cigarettes. Ask occupants of other cars to do the same. Make a note of the codes on the vehicle's hazard labels (see page 18), so you can pass them to the emergency services. Make sure uninjured people wait well away from the vehicle, where the wind won't blow dangerous substances towards them.

- Injured people shouldn't be moved (except for the minimum necessary to carry out first aid) unless they're in immediate danger from fire or explosion. Don't remove a motorcyclist's helmet unless it's essential.

- If anyone's seriously injured, call the emergency services, or make sure someone else has done. If on a motorway, use the emergency telephone, not a mobile phone: it'll help the emergency services to pinpoint you. Give the location as precisely as possible, and (as far as you have them) give brief details of the injuries.

- Administer first aid if necessary (see pages 19 to 20).

- Stay at the scene until the emergency services arrive.

- Make a note of what happened. Sign it and add the date and time. Keep it so you can refer to it if you act as a witness later.

What to note down when you witness an accident

☐ The date, the time, the place.

For each vehicle involved:

☐ The driver's name, address and phone number.

☐ The owner's name and address (if different).

☐ The registration number, make, model and colour of the car.

☐ The insurance company and policy number.

For each witness:

☐ Name, address and phone number.

If the police attended:

☐ Name of officer and station.

Details of the accident:

☐ Sketch the road layout and mark any road signs nearby.

☐ Mark the final position of vehicles, any skid marks or debris on the road.

☐ Note or mark on your sketch the damage to the vehicles.

☐ Note or mark on your sketch the paths travelled by the vehicles, and estimate their speed.

☐ Note the weather conditions and any significant factors (e.g. road condition, obstructions).

☐ If you have a camera to hand, take a photo!

If you're involved in an accident

General advice on what to do at the scene of an accident is on pages 12/13.

If no-one else is injured, and you've caused no damage to any car or property other than your own:

- Check whether your car is in a safe and legal condition. If in any doubt, don't drive it. Call a breakdown service and have it checked over and/or towed to a garage.

- If your car's in a driveable state, decide whether you feel physically and mentally fit to drive. Allow yourself ample time to recover. If in doubt, call for assistance.

- Make a note of what happened, sign, date and time it. If there are any witnesses ask them to sign it too. You can then use it as a reminder if you decide to make a claim on your insurance.

- There's no legal requirement to stop (although it's normally advisable) and you don't have to notify the police.

- If you're unsure whether to claim the cost of repairs, ask first for an estimate so you can compare it with the likely effect on your no-claim bonus. If you plan to claim, don't put work in hand without consulting your insurance company first.

If another person's injured, or property or a vehicle other than your own is damaged, or a farm animal (a horse, cattle, ass, mule, sheep, pig, goat or dog) not in your own vehicle or trailer is killed or injured:

- Keep calm and say as little as possible. However clear the rights and wrongs may be, don't indicate that you accept the blame for the accident. It isn't helpful to show anger or throw accusations at other parties.

- Follow the general guidelines on pages 12/13.

- It's a legal requirement that you stop and remain at the scene for a reasonable period of time (generally, until the emergency services arrive, and/or until other parties have obtained all necessary information).

- It's not a legal requirement that you call the police. Be aware that if the police do attend, they're liable to breathalyse all the drivers involved, regardless of whether they're to blame for the accident.

- Note down all relevant information about the accident (see page 13).

- It's a legal requirement that you give your vehicle registration number, your name and address, and the name and address of the vehicle's owner (if you don't own it) to anyone with reasonable grounds to ask for the information. It's also a legal requirement that you give your insurance details to any person who may hold you responsible for the accident.

- If another person's injured, it's a legal requirement that you produce your certificate of insurance to the police or to any other person who has reasonable grounds to require you to produce it.

- If you don't give your name and address at the time of the accident, you must report the accident to the police as soon as reasonably practicable, and in any case within twenty-four hours. (This is a maximum period and you should not deliberately take that long.)

If any other person's injured and you do not produce your insurance certificate at the time of the accident, it is a legal requirement that you:

- report the accident to the police as soon as possible, and in any case within 24 hours, and

- produce your insurance certificate to the police, either when reporting the accident or within seven days at a police station you can select when reporting the accident.

If the police stop you

The police have wide powers to stop drivers, inspect cars and ask to see documents. Assume if you're stopped by an uniformed police officer, s/he is within his/her rights. Stay calm, and be polite at all times. Co-operate with the inspection of your car. If asked to show documents (generally your driving licence, MOT certificate and certificate of insurance) do so, if you have them with you. (If you don't, you'll probably be required to produce them at a police station within seven days.)

The police don't have powers to breathalyse motorists at random. An uniformed police officer can however ask you to take a breath test if you are or have been driving or attempting to drive a car, or are or have been in charge of a car (without necessarily driving it) provided:

- either the police officer has reasonable cause to suspect you've been drinking.

- or you've committed a moving traffic offence (for example speeding, dangerous driving, ignoring a road sign).

- or it's at the scene of an accident. A driver at the scene of an accident can be (and currently the policy is that s/he will be) breathalysed regardless of whether they committed an offence or were at fault.

If you're stopped by a police officer any of the following may happen.

The police officer may decide you haven't committed any offence. When told to, you can drive on.

The police officer may find there's an illegal defect to your car (e.g. a light not working). Depending on the nature of the defect, s/he could:

- give you a verbal warning. No other action will follow. You can drive on (unless ordered otherwise) but it's wise to have the defect remedied asap.

- issue a VDRS notice (see page 88) requiring you to remedy the defect as soon as possible, and return the form within 14 days. If you comply with the procedure you won't be won't found guilty of any offence relating to the defect, although it doesn't make you immune from being stopped for the same defect again.

- issue a fixed penalty notice. You can either pay the penalty within 28 days, or ask to have the offence dealt with in court. (The notice tells you how to do this.) Unless you have a defence against the charge, or there are strong mitigating circumstances so you believe the penalty is unjustified, you're normally well advised to pay the penalty (which amounts to pleading guilty). Remedy the defect quickly, or you could be stopped and charged again.

- report you for a summons. You don't have to go to the police station, but you'll later receive a summons through the post. This means you'll be tried for the offence and may be found guilty and penalised. You don't have to attend court unless you plead not guilty. Remedy the defect promptly, or you could be stopped and charged again. If the car's dangerous to drive, although the police officer won't detain you, don't drive it again until the fault's corrected.

The police officer may decide you've committed a moving traffic offence. Depending on the nature and seriousness of the offence, s/he could:

- give you a verbal warning. No other action will follow. You can drive on provided you won't commit a further offence by doing so. (This could happen, for instance, if you jump a red light.)

- issue a fixed penalty notice (as above). When told to, you can drive on provided you won't be committing a further offence. (This might happen for example if you're caught speeding.) You won't be issued with a fixed penalty notice if the police officer has seen your licence and noticed that under the totting-up rules (see page 89) the penalty points you'll receive make you liable for disqualification. In that case you'll be reported for a summons.

- Report you for a summons, as above. This is the likely action for a moderately serious offence such as careless driving. Of course you won't drive on if your offence is drink-driving, but you can drive on when the police officer releases you, if you won't commit a further offence by doing so. Even if your offence means you're likely to be disqualified, you can continue to drive until the case is heard and the disqualification imposed.

- If the offence is serious, arrest you and take you immediately to a police station. A typical offence which might prompt this is causing death by dangerous driving.

More details of motoring offences and the prescribed penalties for them are on pages 87 to 94.

Hazardous substances

If a vehicle carrying hazardous substances is involved in an accident, it is important to give the emergency services information about the substances involved.

The vehicle should display a plate with standardised Hazchem information similar to this example:

Quote the coded numbers when you ring the emergency services.

These Hazchem symbols will tell you what are the risks to allow for:

 Non-flammable compressed gas

 Toxic substance

 Oxidising substance

 Multi-loads

 Radioactive substance

 Spontaneously combustible substance

 Corrosive substance

First aid

Every driver should know some basic first aid. The advice here is only a short summary, and although it should be helpful, it really is not sufficient to ensure that you take the right action in common situations. It's a good idea to take a first aid course. The St. John Ambulance Association and Brigade, St. Andrew's Ambulance Association and The British Red Cross Society are good sources of advice and training.

The first aid kit

Always carry a first aid kit in your car. You can buy one ready-assembled (choose one designed for motorists) or create your own if you prefer.

It should contain the following basic essentials:

- A pair of disposable gloves.
- Triangular bandages.
- A large sterile dressing for treating burns or major bleeding.
- Plasters for cuts and grazes.
- Antiseptic wipes for cleaning small wounds.

Also very useful are:

- Plastic bags (sandwich bags are ideal) for enclosing dressed hand or arm burns.
- Safety pins for fastening bandages.
- A small pair of round-nosed scissors for trimming bandages or cutting away clothing.
- A container of water (not for drinking, but for cooling burns and making cold compresses).

Check over your kit at regular intervals (say, when your car is serviced) and replace any items that are used or damaged.

The basic rules

- If you suspect there are serious casualties, your first priority is to ensure that the emergency services are called.
- Work as rapidly as you can but don't rush or run and do not panic.
- Don't put yourself or other helpers in danger. Ensure all vehicles are securely stationary before you enter them.
- Quickly assess the casualties and see to the most seriously injured first. Never assume anyone is dead. Persist with first aid until the emergency services arrive.

- Avoid moving casualties any more than is essential to remove them from serious danger (from traffic, hazardous fumes, etc.).

- Keep casualties warm with blankets or extra clothing, but don't give them food or drink.

- Don't remove a motorcyclist's helmet unless it's necessary to control bleeding or free their airway.

- Don't pull foreign bodies out of wounds.

Urgent priorities

- The first priority is to ensure that the victim is able to breathe. Make sure that their airway is not obstructed by anything (including false teeth). Gently tilt their head backwards to open the airway.

- If the victim isn't breathing, attempt to resuscitate them by performing artificial ventilation. Lift their jaw and pinch their nose shut (unless it's a small child, in which case let your mouth surround their mouth and nose). Put your lips around their mouth and breathe out for about two seconds. Move your mouth away, give the victim's chest time to fall, then repeat until they're breathing unaided.

- If there's severe external bleeding, try to stanch it. Apply pressure to the wound (avoiding any foreign bodies), and bandage a sterile dressing (or the best available alternative) securely in place. Raise unbroken limbs above the level of the victim's heart.

- Unconscious victims are safest in the recovery position, lying on their front with one arm and leg bent to raise their body slightly, and with their head to one side.

Dealing with shock

- The victim is best in a sheltered place, perhaps in a car not involved in the accident. If they're in the open, ensure they're covered warmly (and not sitting or lying directly on the cold ground).

- Loosen tight clothing and give them space to breathe.

- Keep them still, preferably sitting or lying down.

- Give honest reassurance and ensure that expert help is called.

The
paperwork

The driving licence

In order to drive a car on the public highway in the UK you must have one of the following:

- a signed valid provisional driving licence (in which case you must be accompanied: see page 115).

- a signed valid full driving licence.

- in some circumstances, you may use a signed valid International Driving Permit for up to a year after your entry to the UK.

- a full driving licence issued by another country.

How many of us drive?
In 1993-5 81.1% of men and 55.5% of women had a full car driving licence

Young drivers

In the UK the minimum age for car drivers is 17, unless you receive a mobility allowance, in which case you can drive at 16. In many countries you aren't allowed to drive until you're 18, so 17 year olds can't drive even if they have a UK licence. For some categories of larger vehicle, you must be 18 or 21.

What you can drive

Your licence indicates the classes of vehicle you are licensed to drive, and any restrictions on the class (for instance, automatics only, or non-commercial uses only).

Until January 1997 the basic car driving test entitled you to a licence to drive not only cars, but also small lorries with a gross weight up to 7.5 tonnes (7.38 tons approx), and minibuses with up to 16 passenger seats provided you were not driving them not for hire or reward. You were also entitled to draw trailers (with some restrictions) behind any of these vehicles. In January 1997 the licence was changed to a new EC model, and now the basic car licence limits drivers to vehicles under 3.5 tonnes (3.44 tons approx) and with less than eight passenger seats.

If you still have a licence issued before 1997, you can continue to drive all the classes of vehicle listed on your licence. If your licence expires and is replaced, though, the new licence will entitle you to drive only the new limited classes of vehicle.
If you want to extend it, you'll need to make an application to the DVLA, and will have to pass a medical examination.

The cost
At the time of writing the fees for licences were:

First provisional licence	£21
Changing a provisional for your first full licence	Free
Duplicate licence if yours is lost or stolen	£6
Replacement licence to change your class entitlement or remove endorsements	£6

If you're disqualified
When your disqualification finishes, you need to apply for a new licence. The cost is normally £12. If you were disqualified for some drink driving offences, the cost is £20. If your penalty specified that you had to take a new driving test before driving again, then you need to get a provisional licence (cost £12). When you pass the test, it'll cost you a further £6 for your full licence.

If it's endorsed
Once your conviction has expired, you can have the endorsement taken off your licence. Apply to the DVLA for a replacement.

Can you drive without a licence?
You can't drive while you're waiting for your first provisional licence to arrive. (It can take up to three weeks.)

But if you've held a licence before and send it off to obtain a replacement, then you're allowed to drive in the period until the replacement is delivered.

The Vehicle Registration Document and number plates

The V5, or Vehicle Registration Document, shows the registered keeper of a vehicle – the person who keeps the vehicle on a public road. S/he might not be the legal owner: for example, your daughter might drive a car you own, registered in her name.

The V5 was redesigned in 1997 and is now a three-part form. The blue section is sent to the DVLA when changes are made to the registration details (e.g. when you buy or sell a car). The green section is held by the new keeper of the car, as a temporary document until the DVLA issues a revised complete form. The red section is used only when buying or selling through a motor trader.

When and how to register

Brand new cars are normally registered by the dealer you buy from. When you buy a used car from a private buyer, it's your responsibility to ensure that the car's re-registered in your name.

Don't wait until you need to renew the car tax. Normally you do this by completing the relevant section of the existing V5, but if you don't have a V5 you can apply for one, using a form available from Post Offices and Vehicle Registration Offices (VROs). (The DVLA can provide the addresses of VROs.)

Use the V5 to inform the DVLA:

- as soon as you sell your vehicle, either privately or to a motor trader (who may agree to do this for you).

- if you change the colour, engine, fuel type, cylinder capacity, or seating capacity of your car (or weight if you have a goods vehicle).

- if your car is written off or scrapped.

- if you plan to export your car for more than 12 months.

You don't need to inform the DVLA if your car's stolen. You tell the police and they tell the DVLA.

Registering your car isn't the same as licensing it

although both are legal requirements if your car is on the road (and registering is desirable even if it's not). Licensing your car is done by paying for a tax disc: see pages 26/7.

Checking the details

Check the details on the V5 carefully when you buy a car, and ensure that they match the car itself. Note particularly the chassis and engine numbers which uniquely identify that car, and check them against the numbers on the car.

You'll need to satisfy yourself independently that the seller actually owns the car – for instance, by seeing a bill of sale transferring it to him/her, or a hire purchase discharge document.

Details of only the current and one previous keeper are shown on the V5, but the form tells you how many keepers there have been in all. Those with reason to know can obtain information about earlier keepers from the DVLA for a small fee (currently £5).

Where to keep the V5

In a safe place, but not in the car itself, or you'll make it easy for a thief. When you travel abroad you'll need to take it with you, but keep it in a handbag or briefcase which you take with you when you leave your car.

Importing a car to the UK

If you import a car from abroad, you must register and licence it in the UK as soon as possible after it arrives in the country. You can apply to do this at a suitable VRO. You'll then be given a British registration and a vehicle excise licence.

Number plates

There are detailed regulations governing the design, manufacture and display of vehicle registration plates (number plates). In general it's an offence to display mis-spaced registrations or to tamper with the plate so as to make numbers look like letters, or vice versa.

The prefixes are changing

From 1998 the letter prefix to standard number plates will change twice a year, rather than once. When 'Z' is reached the system will change again.

Custom registrations

If you want a customised number plate, be prepared to pay heavily. You can find numbers available for transfer through small ads in the motoring press, or buy some direct from the DVLA. More details of available plates, and rules about their transfer, are available on the DVLA registration hotline – 0181 200 6565.

Road tax and the tax disc

It's a legal requirement on the owners or operators of almost all road vehicles in the UK to pay the correct vehicle excise duty and display a tax disc on the front windscreen. This applies whether you drive the car, or simply leave it parked on a public highway. There are a few exempt classes of specialist vehicle. Cars more than 25 years old are also exempt from payment, but must display a disc. Some disabled people are exempt – further information is available from the DSS Benefits Section.

The tax disc is specific to the vehicle and shows its registration number. It can't be transferred to another vehicle.

How to tax your car

Normally the dealer obtains the first licence for a new car. If the car you bought isn't already licensed, apply yourself on a V55 application form.

The tax can be paid either yearly or half-yearly. There's a 10% handling fee if you pay half-yearly. Each time the licence needs renewing, you must complete an application form and submit an application (by post or in person), either to a post office or to a Vehicle Registration Office. You can't apply direct to the DVLA.

When licensing your car you must produce (as well as the application form and your payment):

- your Vehicle Registration Document (or if you don't have one, a form V62).

- a valid Certificate of Insurance.

- an MOT test certificate if the car is more than three years old.

If you buy a used car the seller might include the unexpired part of the licence in the sale. If not, then it's up to you to apply for a new licence.

If your car's off the road
and on private property all the time, you don't need a licence. Apply for a new licence not more than two working days before you want it to come into effect.

Driving a car without a licence
is usually an offence, but you're allowed to do it when driving to and from a testing station for an MOT test for which you've previously fixed an appointment. You're also allowed (not in law, but as a concession) to use the car for up to 14 days after the licence expires, provided you apply for a new licence (which will run on from the expiry date of the last one) within that period.

Getting a refund
If you've paid for complete months of road tax you won't be using (for example, if the car's a write-off) you can apply for a

refund. You can do this even if you've lost the tax disc (or had it stolen with the car). Get a form V14 from a VRO or Post Office, and send it off to the DVLC Refund Section.

The MOT certificate

If your car's over three years old (its age is measured either from when it was first registered, or if it wasn't registered immediately, from the end of the year of manufacture) it must pass an annual MOT test. (Some other vehicles must be tested after one year.) The test is done by a Vehicle Testing Station appointed by the Vehicle Inspectorate. In 1996-7 there were 18,565 of them, mostly private garages.

You can only drive without a valid MOT:

- to the Testing Station to take the test (by prior arrangement).

- away from the station, after failing.

- to a garage where you have arranged to have the defects noted in a test failure corrected.

To avoid a gap, you can take your car for testing up to a month before the current certificate expires. The new one lasts a year from the expiry date of the old one, not from the date of testing.

More details on what's covered in the MOT test are on pages 34 to 47.

Insurance

The law

Under the Road Traffic Act 1988 Third Party insurance is compulsory. It must cover both the car and the driver. Third Party insurance won't recompense you if your car is damaged or stolen. However if you're at fault in an accident where another person is injured, or another car damaged, the other person can claim on it.

The details of your insurance are summarised on an insurance certificate. The certificate must by law be produced:

- if you're asked to show it by an uniformed police officer.

- if you're involved in an accident.

- when you tax your car.

If you take out insurance at short notice, the insurer may issue you with a cover note. This provides evidence that you have the legal minimum of insurance coverage for a limited time until all the details have been agreed, and the insurance certificate issued.

It's not compulsory to have Fire or Theft coverage, but the usual basic option available from insurance companies is for Third Party, Fire and Theft.

Utmost good faith

The law governing insurance works on the principle of utmost good faith: the insured tells the insurer all about the risk being covered. Any suggestion that you've misrepresented the risk can invalidate your insurance. For this reason it's essential to tell your insurer about any change which could affect the risk – including, for instance, a change of address or in your type of work. It's also essential that you tell the insurer when you have an accident – even if you don't plan to make a claim.

Claiming on Third Party insurance

- If you're involved in an accident and aren't at fault, you can claim on the other driver's insurance. Even if you're not certain who's at fault, always ask for details of coverage from all other drivers involved. First though, talk to your own insurer (either direct, or through your broker if that's how you took out the policy). Often it's best to let them make the claim for you.

- The damage to your car may be covered under two policies, your own and the other driver's. Insurance companies have a complex set of agreements (too complex to summarise here) which determine which policy pays up when, and whether your no-claim bonus is affected.

- The other person may be liable for expenses that aren't covered under your own policy: for example, your loss of earnings while you're injured, or the cost of hiring a car while yours is off the road. Pursuing a claim against another driver can be expensive, though. It's possible to obtain legal expenses insurance (your motor policy may include it, or offer it as an extra) to cover the costs.

- No excess operates on Third Party insurance, so you or your insurers can claim against the other driver for the amount of any excess on your own policy.

If the other driver isn't insured
The Motor Insurers' Bureau provides a central fund (funded by motor insurers) to compensate the victims of accidents where the drivers are uninsured or untraced.

Comprehensive insurance
The term 'comprehensive' generally applies to insurance that covers damage to your own vehicle. It'll cover the damage regardless of whether you're at fault. However no insurance is entirely comprehensive, and the coverage under different policies can vary widely. In choosing an insurer it's worth looking at the following aspects:

- The insurance may cover just one driver, or several named drivers, or any driver. (The wider, the more expensive.)

- There may be an excess: the insurer won't pay say the first £100 of any claim.

- Check how restricted the insurer is in their repairing arrangements, and whether they provide an accident recovery service (to retrieve you and your car after an accident, and take the car to the repairer).

- Check whether the insurer will provide a courtesy car while yours is off the road.

- Coverage for driving abroad can vary. Check whether you automatically have cover as comprehensive as in the UK, or whether you'll have to obtain extra cover when you travel. And check whether there's an upper limit for the amount of time you and/or your car can spend abroad.

- Check on the extent of coverage when you drive cars other than your own.

Some policies cover your legal costs if you're charged with a motoring offence. Hopefully you'll never need it, but if you do, it'll save you a lot of money.

Changing your life/ changing your car: who to tell

	Driving Licence DVLA	Vehicle Registration DVLA	Your Insurer
When you move house	Yes (legal requirement)	Yes (legal requirement)	Yes – or your coverage may be void
When you change jobs			Yes – or your coverage may be void
When you change your name	Yes (legal requirement)	Yes (legal requirement)	Advisable
If you have an accident		Not unless your car is changed significantly when rebuilt, or it's a write-off	Your first claim is on your own insurance. If you decide not to claim, you should still give details of any accidents you've had when renewing your insurance, or your coverage may be void
If you're charged with a motoring offence			Yes – or your coverage may be void
If you buy or import a car to the UK		Yes (legal requirement)	Yes – Third Party coverage is a legal requirement
If you sell your car		Yes (legal requirement)	Yes – to cancel or amend your cover
If your make significant physical changes to your car		Yes (legal requirement)	Yes – or your coverage may be void
If your car is written-off or scrapped		Yes (legal requirement)	Yes – to cancel or amend your cover
If your car is stolen		(The police will advise them)	Yes
If you lose the document	Yes - you must get a replacement	Yes – you must get a replacement	Yes – you must get a replacement

Keeping your
car in shape

Basic checks on your car's condition

All these items need regular checking, and you don't need to be a mechanic to do it. Make checks before any long journey, and as a routine at least weekly. The fuel level and the general condition of your tyres are worth checking at least daily. Advice on the levels required, and on how to do the checks, should be included in your car handbook.

These basic checks are supplementary to the regular cleans which you'll give your car, and to the regular services which your car will need. Unless you're a skilled mechanic yourself, you're well advised to have your car serviced by a reputable mechanic at the recommended service intervals. It'll not only ensure your car runs safely and economically, it'll also help to maintain its resale value. Using an authorised dealer for your make of car may be a little more expensive than going to a backstreet garage, but it'll give you an advantage when you come to sell your car.

Fuel

- Check the level before setting out. Try not to let the fuel run too low. As well as the risk of running out of fuel completely,

you could also get sediment in the engine as the tank is drained to its very bottom. Ensure that you refill with the correct type of fuel for your car.

Brakes

- It's a good idea to test the brakes every day, by braking firmly on a safe stretch of road, shortly after you set out. Consult your garage if the brakes don't work smoothly, silently and without pulling the car over to one side. Check the level of brake fluid in the fluid reservoir regularly, and seek expert advice if it's below the guideline.

Oil

- Make sure the car isn't on a slope when you check the oil level, or you'll get a false reading. Check the oil when the engine's cold. Use the dipstick to find the level. (The car handbook will tell you where to locate it.) Withdraw the dipstick, wipe it with a clean cloth, replace it and remove again to check the level.

- Don't top up the oil above the recommended maximum level, or you'll create excess pressure which is bad for the engine. Use the type of oil recommended for your car.

- Never continue to drive when the oil is at a very low level, or you could do irreparable damage to the engine.

Water
- Check the level of coolant in the cooling system. In older cars this is done by removing the radiator cap. In newer cars there's usually an expansion tank or header tank. The car handbook will advise you on the level to maintain. Don't remove the radiator cap when the engine is hot, or you risk being scalded, and don't add cold water to an overheated engine, or you could damage it. Let it cool down first.

- In cold weather, the cooling system should hold a mixture of water and antifreeze. It's important to maintain the strength of the antifreeze when topping up, by using a similar mixture.

- If you have the kind of battery that can be topped up, check the level of water in the battery.

- Check the level of screen wash in the bottle and top it up if necessary.

Tyre condition and pressure
- Check the pressures of front, back and spare tyres, and add air if necessary to obtain the correct pressure. The car handbook will advise you on the pressures required, which may vary depending on the load you carry. The air pressure gauges at garages are not always accurate, and you may find it more satisfactory to invest in a portable gauge, with or without a handpump attached.

- Check all tyres regularly for any signs of damage, and for excessive or uneven wear. A tyre depth gauge is useful. Worn tyres should be replaced before they reach the legal minimum tread. A too broad or narrow pattern of wear is a sign that the tyre is under- or over-pressurised. Irregular patterns indicate that the wheel alignment needs checking.

Lamps and indicators
- Check all lights and indicators are working properly, and replace any broken bulbs. You'll need another person to help you check that the brake lights work properly when the main brake's applied.

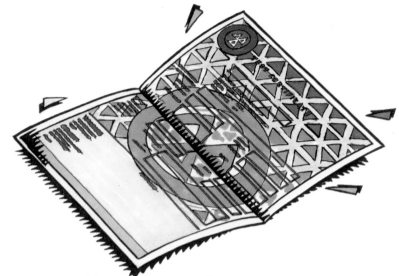

Legal requirements and the MOT test

Legal requirements and the MOT test

The next few pages outline the general legal requirements applying to the fabric of your car. They also explain in general terms what the MOT test covers. There are many precise requirements and special exceptions which can't be covered here: your garage or dealer can give you advice on the regulations applying to your particular car.

The MOT test was designed to ensure that cars are safe and environmentally sound. It's not particularly intended to ensure that their performance is at its peak, or that they maintain their value. Passing the MOT is a basic requirement for your car once it is more than three years old, but doing the minimum necessary to get your car through its MOT isn't a good substitute for full regular servicing.

The MOT is not a road test. Normally it's carried out in a garage. Parts of it require special equipment or inspection pits, but many of the items checked by the MOT tester can also be checked by the independent motorist.

Lights

Modern cars are required to have a variety of lights fitted. (The requirements are a little looser for older cars.) The MOT tests virtually all the lights on a car, sometimes including optional lights where they're fitted.

General requirements are that all the obligatory lights are in place. All lights must be securely fixed, the switch operating them must work properly, and they must be clean and in good working order. They mustn't flicker, or go out when tapped lightly by hand. They mustn't be too damaged to work properly, although it's permissible for a light to be repaired if the repair is secure and durable and the light continues to work acceptably.

Headlamps

Most cars must legally have two headlamps. There are some exceptions, for example for cars first used before 1 January 1931. There should be a matched pair of main beam headlamps and a matched pair of dipped beam headlamps. Often the two will be within the same unit. 'Matched pair' means that the two must be of the same size and shape, and that they must give out light of substantially the same colour and density. The light must be either white or yellow. The precise position isn't specified, but they should be at about the same height and distance from the side of the car. The MOT also checks the aim of the headlamps on both main and dipped beam. There are detailed guidelines designed to ensure that main beams are on or slightly below the horizontal, and that dipped lights aim to the left and don't dazzle. If a second pair of headlamps are fitted, their aim must be correct too. 'Converter' kits are allowable for right-hand drive cars, so long as the converter or mask is securely fixed and the light output isn't reduced too much.

Front and rear position lamps

These are legally required on virtually all cars. The front lights must show a steady white light (or a steady yellow light, if they're incorporated in a yellow-light headlamp) and the rear lights a steady red light.

The MOT test also checks that they're positioned so at least half of each lamp can be seen from the front or rear respectively.

Lights, reflectors and indicators

Brake lights

Two brake lights are legally required on all vehicles first used on or after 1st January 1971. (They're not always required on older vehicles.) They must give out a red light, and be positioned so at least half of each lamp can be seen from the rear of the car. Any additional brake lights are also tested in the MOT.

The MOT test checks that the brake lights go on when the service brake is applied, and that they go off when it's released. It also checks that they aren't affected by the working of other lights on the vehicle. On older cars (pre September 1965) it's allowable for a brake light to double as an indicator, but this isn't permissible on newer cars.

Number plate lights

The rear registration plate must be illuminated when the sidelights are switched on. If there's more than one bulb, then they must all be working. The MOT checks that the number plate light goes on when the sidelights are on, and as with all other lights, that it's in good working order and gives out a steady light.

Rear fog lamps

Cars first used on or after 1st April 1980 must have a rear fog lamp fitted, on the centre or offside. There may be more than one fog lamp, but only the mandatory one is tested. It must give out a red light.

The MOT checks that the fog lamp works when dipped headlights are on and the ignition is switched on. It also checks on the working of the 'tell-tale', the dashboard light (or similar) which tells the driver when the fog lamp is on.

Rear reflectors

It's obligatory for two red reflectors to be fitted to the back of the car, one on either side. It's not allowable to use reflective tape as a substitute, and the reflectors must be properly visible and in good working order.

Direction indicators and hazard warning lights

There are complex regulations specifying when indicators and hazard warning lights are required on cars of different ages. New cars must have one side repeater indicator on each side and a hazard warning device.

The indicators must work properly in connection with their switch. They must give out an amber light, except on cars first used before 1 September 1965, which can use white front and red rear indicators. The MOT also checks the flashing rate, which must be between 60 and 120 times per minute. (Old-style 'semaphore' arms, though they must light up, don't have to flash.)

In most circumstances there should be a driver's tell-tale, which could be a noise rather than (or as well as) a light. This too must be in working order.

The MOT checks that the hazard warning device causes all the indicators to flash in phase with each other. It must operate whether the ignition is switched on or off. It should have a separate tell-tale which again is also checked.

Brakes

The handbrake

It's a requirement for all except veteran (pre 1905) cars to have a handbrake or parking brake. It should immobilise at least two wheels on a four-wheeled car. There are thorough regulations in the MOT test to ensure that the handbrake is in good working order and that it will hold the car securely.

The footbrake

There are complex and detailed tests in the MOT to ensure that the footbrake, or service brake, is working properly. There are various different types of braking system, and the regulations vary depending on the type of brake used.

The MOT checks that the brake pedal is in good condition, its anti-slip face is not missing or too worn, and it operates correctly without excessive movement to the side. It checks all rods, cables and other parts of the braking system, and requires that they are all in good condition and not worn or damaged. In systems with

a brake fluid reservoir, the reservoir itself must be in good order and securely fixed, with a functioning reservoir cap. It must not leak, and the fluid must be at the right level.

As well as testing the physical condition of the brake system components, the MOT includes a practical test of the system performance. The test is designed to ensure that the brakes work efficiently, and evenly across all the wheels to which they are applied.

Finally, the MOT checks the rear brake warning light and the tell-tale which lets the driver know that the brakes are in operation.

Young people have the oldest cars

Only 18% of drivers aged 16-29 have a car less than 3 years old, while 22% of them have one over 10 years old. 28% of drivers aged 60-64 have relatively new cars, while only 15% have a car more than ten years old.

Steering, suspension and bodywork

Steering
The MOT test checks that the steering wheel is in good condition and that there isn't excessive play in it. The locking device is checked to ensure that it's in place and secure. Among mechanical checks, the test checks that the steering system functions properly without fouling other components, through from left lock to right lock. If there's power steering, checks are made to ensure it's working properly and the system is free of leaks. (It's allowable to have a power steering system properly disconnected.)

Suspension
Both front and rear suspensions are checked to ensure that they have enough clearance from the chassis or bump stop, and that there's no corrosion of the car frame which could weaken the suspension. The components of the system are checked to ensure they're in good condition and working order. The wheel bearings are checked to ensure there's no excessive movement or tightness. When shock absorbers are standard items on a car, they must be fitted, secure and in good condition.

Bodywork

The main MOT checks to the bodywork are to ensure that it is secure and not dangerous. If there are modifications or there's corrosion which affects the braking or steering or the overall integrity of the car, the MOT inspector will fail the car. However, the MOT is much more lenient with corrosion of parts of the body that aren't structurally important – although rust in these areas too will worry you as a car owner!

Sharp edges which could injure or damage others aren't allowable. The doors must shut securely, and the front doors must be openable from both inside and outside the car. The boot lid or tailgate must also close securely. Front seats are checked to make sure they're secure, and all seats checked to ensure their backrests can be secured in the normal upright position.

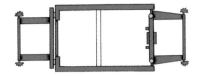
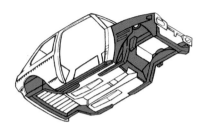

These are the structurally important areas of a typical saloon car

Why Cars Fail the MOT

These were the main reasons for MOT failure, for cars and other passenger vehicles, in 1996/7 (in percentages of all vehicles taking the test).

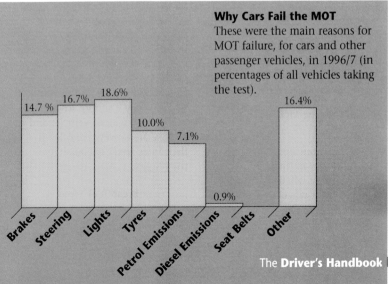

14.7 % Brakes
16.7% Steering
18.6% Lights
10.0% Tyres
7.1% Petrol Emissions
0.9% Diesel Emissions
Seat Belts
16.4% Other

Wheels and tyres

Types of tyre

Radial tyres are now most common. In this type of tyre manufacture, the cords run at right angles across the tyre. In the alternative cross ply design, the cords run diagonally in a layered alternating structure. It's advisable to have the same type of tyre on all wheels, and for the spare wheel. Although it's acceptable to have cross-ply tyres on the front wheels and radial tyres at the back, it is not safe and not acceptable to the MOT tester to have either:

- radial tyres on the front wheels and cross-ply at the rear (regardless of whether your car has front-wheel or rear-wheel drive).

- or, mixed cross-ply and radial-ply tyres on the same axle.

The MOT tester will also check that your tyres are of the same nominal size and aspect ratio. They'll assess whether the tyres are of adequate size, ply and speed rating for the kind of car, but they won't reject a car if the tyres appear inadequate for the type of motoring you might do (for example, if they're remoulds which couldn't handle high speeds): they'll simply advise you of that. (Goods vehicles and the like are however rejected if their tyres aren't adequate for the purpose.)

Breadth of Tread

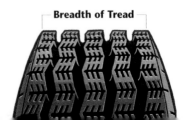

The tread

Tyres must have a continuous tread depth of at least 1.6 mm (0.07 inches approx) on cars, light vans and light trailers (1 mm (0.04 inches approx) for other vehicles) across the centre three-quarters of the width. The tread must be at least visible across the remaining shoulder bands. The MOT test will check that this is the case, but you should also check it yourself at regular intervals. A tyre tread gauge will give you an accurate reading. Many tyres now have built-in tread-wear indicators (TWIs) which become visible once the tread depth is down to the legal minimum, so if you see the indicator it's time to replace your tyre.

General condition

Tyres must also be free from cuts and other defects, and the MOT test will check that this is the case. A cut deep enough to reach the ply or cords, or a limp, bulge or tear, or any other damage which exposes the ply or cord, will cause your car to fail – and of course it will also make the car dangerous to drive.

The MOT test doesn't check the spare tyre, but it is in your interest to ensure that the spare tyre is also in good condition.

Tyre pressures

Checking that tyres are properly inflated isn't part of the MOT test, although a completely flat tyre will affect other aspects of the test (for example, the headlight alignment test) and may cause the car to fail. You should check your tyre pressure frequently, using a reliable gauge and topping up as necessary.

Looking after your tyres

Your tyres will last longer, and your car will drive better and more economically, if you:

- check regularly that the tyres are at the correct pressure. Check when the engine's cold, and ensure that the gauge you use is reliable.

- avoid driving over potholes or raised kerbs.

- avoid scraping the sides of the tyre, for example on kerbs when parking.

- avoid hitting kerbs or other obstructions, which can also affect the tracking of the front wheels.

Centre ¾ of tyre not less than 1.6 mm Tread Depth

The exhaust system and emission requirements

The MOT test doesn't directly check components of the car engine, but there are increasingly stringent requirements regarding exhaust emissions, and it's necessary for your engine to be tuned and running properly in order to meet the standards. If the engine idles at a speed clearly above its normal idling speed, this too is a reason for failure.

It's a legal requirement that a silencer is fitted which reduces the noise of the car engine to an acceptable level. The MOT test checks that both exhaust and silencer are complete, in good working order, and securely mounted to the car. It checks for leaks in the exhaust system. It also checks that the silencer works effectively and the noise level isn't higher than might be expected for the type of car.

The emissions regulations

The regulations are complex, and this is no more than a summary of the main points for the major categories of car. If you want your car to do the least damage to the environment, it's important that its emissions should contain the lowest possible level of carbon monoxide and hydrocarbons. Normally if your car passes its MOT but appears to be operating at well below its normal efficiency, the MOT tester will advise you so you can have the engine checked over.

Cars first used before 1 August 1975

At idling speed, the engine mustn't give out dense blue or clearly visible black smoke. It must also not give out excessive smoke during acceleration, so as to obscure the view of other road users. The test specification does accept that some smoke is unavoidable from older cars, and they don't fail the test if they smoke to a normal level.

Cars dating between 1 August 1975 and 31 July 1986

While older cars receive a visual test only, cars of this age and newer are given precise gas analyser tests which measure the emission levels.

- The exhaust must not emit carbon monoxide (CO) at a density of greater than 4.5%.

- It must not emit hydrocarbons at a density of greater than 1200 ppm (parts per million).

Cars dating between 1 August 1986 and 31 July 1992

Post-1992 cars must have a catalytic converter fitted. Some cars of this age have catalytic converters, but they are given a non-catalyst MOT test regardless of whether a catalytic converter is fitted.

The density limit for hydrocarbons remains at 1200 ppm, but the maximum level for carbon monoxide is reduced to 3.5%.

Cars first used after 1 August 1992

Some light cars are subject to the same standard as cars dating between 1986 and 1992. Other cars are subject to a catalyst test, with limits that are specified for each model of car.

Lambda

As well as testing for hydrocarbons and carbon monoxide, the gas analyser tests for catalytic-converter-equipped cars measure the variation from Lambda, which is a stoichiometric air-to-fuel ratio of 14.5:1. If the car's measurement is below the acceptable variation, it means the engine's fuel: air mixture is too rich. If the measurement is above the acceptable variation, then the mixture is too lean.

Other major requirements of the MOT test

Seat belts

The MOT test checks compulsorily-fitted seat belts. If your car has seat belts or other restraints which aren't required by law, they won't be included in the test.

The test ensures that all required seat belts are provided, that they are of the right type, that they are attached securely and in good working order.

The seat belt requirements are complex, but generally speaking all cars first used after 1st January 1965 must have seat belts which restrain the upper part of the body for the driver and 'specified front passenger'. That is the front passenger seat farthest from the driver; if there is a centre front passenger seat there is no requirement for a belt to be provided.

Cars first used after 31st March 1981 must have a lap belt as well as an upper-body (e.g. diagonal) belt.

Cars first used after 31st March 1987 must also have rear seat belts. Where there are two rear seats, either:

- one of them must have a three-point inertia reel belt.

- or both must have either a lap belt, a child restraint belt, a disabled person's belt or a three-point static belt.

Where there are three forward-facing rear seats, at least two of them must have a seat belt. There are various permissible combinations of the different types of restraint.

See pages 52 to 53 for details of regulations about passengers wearing seat belts when the car's being driven.

Windscreen, wipers and washers

It's important that the driver should have a clear view of the road. The MOT test checks this by inspecting the windscreen to ensure that it's clear and undamaged. Particular attention is paid to the area in front of the driver that's swept by windscreen wipers. Significant damage (or over-large stickers) in this area is a reason for failure.

Although temporary windscreens can be useful as an emergency measure, they must be replaced as quickly as possible, and they won't pass the MOT test.

The MOT test checks windscreen wipers and washers to ensure that they function well and clear the windscreen effectively, with particular emphasis again on the driver's view. And a drooping sun visor on the driver's side could also cause your car to fail its MOT.

The horn

A functioning horn is a legal requirement for all except some vintage cars. The MOT test checks that the horn is present, its control operates properly, and it gives out enough sound. Cars first used after 1 August 1973 must have horns whose noise is constant, uniform, and not too harsh or grating.

Mirrors

All cars must have at least one rear view mirror. For cars first used after 1st August 1978 there must be two rear view mirrors, one of which must be an exterior mirror on the driver's side. The second can be either an exterior mirror on the passenger's side, or an interior mirror. The MOT test checks to ensure these mirrors are provided, are clearly visible from the driver's seat, and are in a condition to do their job properly. It doesn't check additional mirrors.

Vans and other vehicles with a restricted view must have an exterior mirror on each side. If you tow a caravan or wide trailer, you should fit exterior mirrors on extended arms so that they give a view beyond the trailer.

Most exterior mirrors are convex. They have a wider field of vision than flat mirrors, but you should be aware that they make vehicles travelling behind you look smaller. This can deceive you into thinking they're farther away than they are.

What to carry in your car

Carry with you (but don't leave in the car):

- [ ] your Certificate of Insurance (or cover note if you're waiting for a certificate to be issued)
- [ ] your driving licence
- [ ] your Vehicle Registration Document (only when driving abroad)
- [ ] money or credit card for use in an emergency
- [ ] phonecard for use in an emergency
- [ ] a set of spare car keys
- [ ] (if you have one) your breakdown service membership card and emergency number.

It's essential to keep in your car all the time:

- [ ] an adequate amount of petrol in the tank (but don't routinely carry spare supplies; an empty can however could be useful)
- [ ] the car manual (but not the car registration document)
- [ ] a biro and some paper (in case of emergencies)
- [ ] a fully inflated spare tyre with legal tread, and a wheel jack
- [ ] a collapsible warning triangle

- [ ] a fire extinguisher (purpose-designed for cars)
- [ ] a good first aid kit
- [ ] spare bulbs and fuses
- [ ] a clean rag.

It's useful to keep in your car all the time:

- [ ] an effective torch (check the battery regularly)
- [ ] an adequate map for each journey you take
- [ ] vinyl tape, wire, tow rope, pliers and jump leads
- [ ] a plastic container of water
- [ ] wet wipes for oily hands
- [ ] a copy of this book.

In winter it's useful to add:

- [ ] a can of de-icer
- [ ] a lock defroster
- [ ] a scraper/wiper and/or sponge
- [ ] a rug or blanket.

If you travel on long journeys, in heavy snow or to remote places:

- [ ] emergency supplies – biscuits, chocolate, a thermos of hot drink
- [ ] a spade and old sacks
- [ ] matches.

In summer it's worth keeping in the car:

- [ ] a pair of sunglasses.

Try to avoid carrying any excess baggage: the weight will affect your fuel consumption.

Driving:
regulations and tips

Stopping distances

On a dry road, a good car with good brakes and tyres and an alert driver will stop in the distances shown. Remember these are shortest stopping distances.

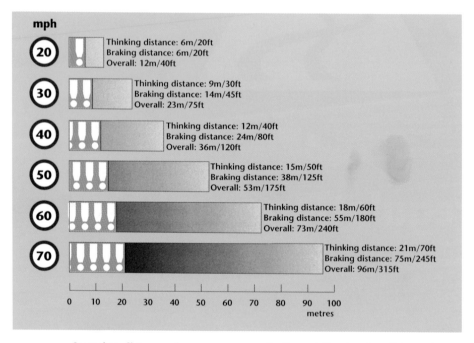

mph

20
Thinking distance: 6m/20ft
Braking distance: 6m/20ft
Overall: 12m/40ft

30
Thinking distance: 9m/30ft
Braking distance: 14m/45ft
Overall: 23m/75ft

40
Thinking distance: 12m/40ft
Braking distance: 24m/80ft
Overall: 36m/120ft

50
Thinking distance: 15m/50ft
Braking distance: 38m/125ft
Overall: 53m/175ft

60
Thinking distance: 18m/60ft
Braking distance: 55m/180ft
Overall: 73m/240ft

70
Thinking distance: 21m/70ft
Braking distance: 75m/245ft
Overall: 96m/315ft

0 10 20 30 40 50 60 70 80 90 100
metres

Stopping distances increase greatly when:

- the road is wet or slippery (with ice, wet leaves, oil spillages, etc.).

- brakes and tyres are substandard.

- the driver is tired or preoccupied.

In the wet the stopping distance is at least twice the distance indicated. On ice it could be more than ten times the distance.

Speed limits

	Built-up areas	Single Carriageways	Dual Carriageways	Motorways
Cars including car-derived vans and motorcycles	30	60	70	70
Cars towing caravans or trailers (including car-derived vans and motorcycles)	30	50	60	60
Buses and coaches less than 12 m long	30	50	60	70
Goods vehicles under 7.5 tonnes max laden weight	30	50	60	70 **60** if articulated or towing a trailer
Goods vehicles over 7.5 tonnes max laden weight	30	40	50	60

Conversion tables are on page 124

These are the national speed limits (in miles per hour) which apply to all roads unless signs show otherwise. The 30 mph limit applies to all traffic on all roads in England and Wales, and Class C and unclassified roads in Scotland, which have street lighting, unless signs show otherwise. Increasingly you will notice 20 mph speed limits in built-up areas, especially near schools and in residential areas where children may be playing. Sometimes these are only advisory limits. Often they're accompanied by physical speed-limiting measures such as chicanes and sleeping policemen, so an additional reason for keeping to the limit is to avoid damaging your car.

When you must wear a seat belt

Wearing seat belts makes good sense, because it has been shown to save lives and reduce the risk of serious injury in an accident. It's also a legal requirement: generally you MUST wear a seat belt if one is available, unless you fall into one of the limited exempt categories.

Inertia reel belts are the safest general option, but static belts are better than no belt. Three-point belts with a lap belt and a diagonal belt across the body are the safest, and are required equipment on some seats. Page 46 outlines which seat belts must be fitted in your car.

An appropriate child restraint is a baby carrier, child seat, harness or booster seat appropriate to the child's weight. An adult belt will be uncomfortable for a child to wear, and unsafe: the belt itself could cause injury, and it's unlikely to restrain a child adequately.

Specially designed belts are available for disabled persons. Ensure that one is fitted if you regularly carry a disabled passenger.

Who's responsible for wearing what when

	Front seat	Rear seat	Whose responsibility
Driver	Must be worn if fitted		Driver
Child under 3 years of age	Appropriate child restraint must be worn	Appropriate child restraint must be worn if available	Driver
Child aged 3 – 11 and under 1.5 metres (about 5ft) in height	Appropriate child restraint must be worn if available. If not, an adult seat belt must be worn	Appropriate child restraint must be worn if available. If not, an adult seat belt must be worn if available	Driver
Child aged 12, 13 or younger child 1.5 metres or more in height	Adult seat belt must be worn if available	Adult seat belt must be worn if available	Driver
Adult passengers	Must be worn if available	Must be worn if available	Passenger

Those exempted from wearing seat belts include:

- holders of medical exemption certificates.

- people making local deliveries in a vehicle designed or adapted for that purpose.

- children in the rear of taxis with partitions.

Who makes an insurance claim

In 1995, private car comprehensive insurance (from insurers other than Lloyds) covered 12.76 million vehicle years (the equivalent of 12.76 million drivers for the full year). There were 2.67 million claims, including claims for fire, theft and accidents, with an average settlement cost of £980.

Private car non-comprehensive covered 4.91 million vehicle years. A smaller percentage of drivers made claims: there were 650,000 in all, with an average settlement cost of £1326.

Lighting up

Pages 34 to 37 outline which lights and indicators are legally required on your car. This section explains when you must use them

It's essential to ensure that all your lights are clean, in good working order, and that your headlights are properly adjusted. Headlights with badly aimed beams can dazzle other road users and may cause accidents. In dirty driving conditions, wipe the surface of the lights regularly. Surface grime can dramatically reduce the amount of light emitted.

If your lights don't work properly, you're breaking the law. Carrying spare bulbs and fuses is a requirement in many countries, and is a wise precaution everywhere.

When to use which lights

- You must use your sidelights (as a minimum) between the hours of sunset and sunrise.

- You must use headlights at night (that is, between half an hour after sunset and half an hour before sunrise) on:

  - all roads without any street lighting.

  - roads where the street lights are more than 185 m (600 ft) apart.

  - roads where street lights are provided but they are not lit up.

  - lit motorways and roads with a speed limit above 50 mph.

- Even where street lights are provided in built-up areas, use dipped headlights if the road is not well lit.

- Use your headlights or your front fog lights (if they're fitted) when visibility is seriously reduced. As a general guide, use fog lights when you can't see clearly for more than 100 m (328 ft). You must not use fog lights at other times: don't treat front fog lights as an extra set of headlights. Remember to switch them off as soon as the visibility improves.

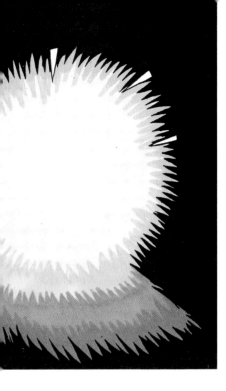

Avoiding glare

It's easy to be dazzled by the full beam headlights of an oncoming car. A car following another can also dazzle the driver when s/he looks in the rear view mirror. Be careful to dip your headlights whenever you might dazzle another driver.

If your vehicle has dim-dip, use that setting instead of full headlights in dull daytime weather and at night in built-up areas with good street lighting.

If you find you're dazzled yourself by the lights of another car, then slow down or stop if possible, until you're able to see clearly again.

Flashing your headlights

The *Highway Code* is adamant that flashing headlights should be used for only one purpose: to let another road user know you're there. Some motoring experts argue that it's time to change the rules, since so many motorists use them as a signal that they're giving way, but that's not the official meaning, and the official advice is that you should use them only for the designated purpose.

Hazard warning lights

Flashing hazard warning lights are used to warn other drivers of an obstruction. Normally you should only use them when your car is stationary. The only time you should use them when driving is when you're on a motorway or unrestricted dual carriageway and you need to warn drivers behind you of a hazard or obstruction ahead. Use the hazard lights sparingly, and only for just long enough to ensure that drivers behind you have heeded the warning. Your brake lights also act as a warning that it's necessary to slow down.

Hazard lights should not be used when you park in a dangerous or illegal place. There's only one message here: don't do it.

Parking

Some of the places where you mustn't park:

- the carriageway of a motorway.

- a slip road to a motorway.

- the hard shoulder of a motorway.

- the central reservation of a motorway.

- a Clearway.

- an Urban Clearway within its hours of operation, except to pick up or set down passengers.

- a road marked with double white lines, even if one of the lines is broken, except to pick up or set down passengers.

- a bus lane, tram lane or a cycle lane marked by an unbroken white line during its period of operation.

- in a parking space reserved for specific users (e.g. Orange Badge holders or residents) unless you're entitled to do so.

- anywhere at night if you're facing against the direction of the traffic flow.

- a Zebra, Puffin or Pelican crossing, including the area marked by zigzag lines.

- where there are parking restrictions in force, as shown by yellow lines along the edge of the carriageway (or red lines on Red Routes). A sign will tell you when the restrictions are in force: it may be near the kerb, or it may be at the entry point to a controlled parking zone.

And some more places where it's inadvisable (and in some circumstances illegal) to park:

- on a footpath, pavement or cycle track.

- near a school entrance.

- at or near a bus stop or taxi rank.

- on the approach to a level crossing.

- within 10 m (32 ft) of a junction, except if you're in an authorised parking space.

- near the brow of a hill or hump bridge.

- opposite a traffic island.

- opposite another parked vehicle if your car might cause an obstruction. (Ask yourself if a fire engine could get through.)

- where you would force other traffic to enter a tram lane.

- where the kerb has been lowered to help wheelchair users.

- in front of the entrance to a property.

Parking at night

The basic rule is that you must leave your sidelights on. You need not use your lights however if you're parked in a road with a speed limit of 30 mph or less, and are:

- at least 10 m (32 ft) away from any junction, close to the kerb and facing in the direction of traffic flow.

- or in a recognised parking space.

Parking offences

The Road Traffic Act (1991) decriminalised most non-endorsable on-street parking offences in London. The local traffic authority is responsible for enforcing parking restrictions, not the police: and if you break them you face inconvenience (your car may be clamped or towed away) and a heavy fine, but not a conviction. Local authorities outside London are allowed to follow suit in some circumstances, and some already have.

Dangerous or seriously obstructive parking is an endorsable offence (there's more on motoring offences on pages 87 to 94) which means it's still liable to lead to prosecution.

Wheel clamping is the best deterrent

According to research by the Metropolitan Police, wheel clamping cuts down illegal parking by more than other enforcement measures. Where it's in force, a study by the TRRI has shown, motorists spent 40% less time parked illegally on yellow lines, and 33% less time parked illegally in residents' parking bays. Towing cars away doesn't give the same visible message to other drivers, and it's more expensive to enforce. But it's the best solution when a car is causing an obstruction.

A small consolation: you won't be clamped until you've gone 15 minutes beyond the paid-for time at a parking meter or in a time-restricted parking place.

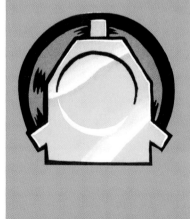

Motorways and giving way

Motorways mustn't be used by:

- pedestrians.
- provisional licence holders.
- slow-moving vehicles.

Reversing on a motorway is forbidden.

The right-hand lane (where there are three or more lanes) mustn't be used except in prescribed circumstances by:

- any vehicle drawing a trailer.
- a goods vehicle with a maximum laden weight over 7.5 tonnes (7.38 tons approx).
- a bus or coach longer than 12 metres (39.4 feet approx).

Reflecting studs

The colour variation is designed to help you orient yourself in the dark.

- White – lane markings, or the middle of the road.
- Red – the edge of the road.
- Amber – by the central reservation of a dual carriageway or motorway.
- Green – across lay-bys and side roads.

Some situations where you must give way

- Turning at road junctions, when a pedestrian is already crossing the road.

- When a pedestrian is walking on a pavement you need to cross, for example to reach a driveway.

- When a pedestrian has stepped out on to a Zebra crossing. (You're not obliged to stop when they're waiting by the roadside, although you will of course be courteous, especially to children, elderly people and people with disabilities.)

- At Pelican crossings when the amber light is flashing after the red light has gone off, if there are any pedestrians still on the crossing. Remember that where there's a central island, a Pelican crossing on both sides of it counts as one crossing, not two, and you must give way to pedestrians crossing the other carriageway.

- On a motorway slip road, you must give way to traffic already on the motorway.

Seeing clearly (or not so clearly)

The legal minimum eyesight for a driver requires them to read a number plate with letters 79.4 mm (3.1 inches) tall at a distance of 20.5 m (67 ft). It's worth checking regularly that you still meet the minimum: recent research by Aston University suggested that 1.2 million drivers on the road fall short of it. Their punishment is to have ten per cent more accidents than the average driver.

Lead is on its way out

From 31st December 1999 an EC Directive will outlaw the sale of leaded petrol. Drivers of cars that only run on leaded petrol will need to use unleaded petrol and add the necessary additives separately.

Children and dogs

It's an offence to let children sit behind the rear seats in an estate car or hatchback.

If your dog comes in the car with you, make sure it's firmly secured – for its and your protection (and for the safety of other motorists). A full-length grille between front and back seats ensures animals can't interfere with your driving. Just as good are harnesses which fix the dog firmly to a seat belt or to a hook fixed on to the car; or use a dog/cat/rabbit hutch or basket, which you can then secure firmly on the seat or floor of the car.

Some estate cars are relatively well equipped with hooks for securing animals and other movable items. Others have dangerous protuberances, which could injure an animal if you stop suddenly. Check the interior carefully if you plan to carry an animal.

Mobile phones

It's dangerous to drive while using a hand-held mobile phone. The police are liable to charge you with careless driving if you do it. It's permissible to use a hands-off phone so long as your concentration is not affected, but lapses in concentration will cost you dearly. However urgent that incoming call, it's not permissible to stop on the hard shoulder of a motorway to take it. Be careful too when changing tapes, CDs and radio stations, and avoid doing it altogether when driving fast.

Cycle lanes and crowded roads

Cycle lanes

It's an offence to drive (or park) in a cycle lane marked by an unbroken white line during its period of operation. It's not an offence to drive in a cycle lane marked by a broken white line, but you shouldn't do so unless it's unavoidable.

The roads are getting more crowded...

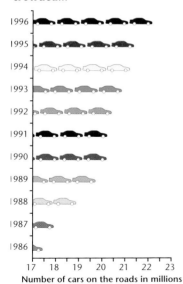

Number of cars on the roads in millions

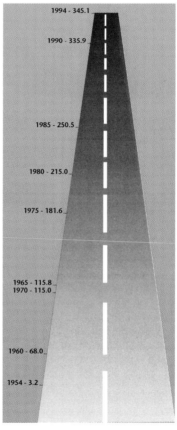

1994 - 345.1
1990 - 335.9
1985 - 250.5
1980 - 215.0
1975 - 181.6
1965 - 115.8
1970 - 115.0
1960 - 68.0
1954 - 3.2

Total length of car and taxi journeys in the UK each year, by billion vehicle kilometres

Towing a caravan or trailer

If you plan to tow any kind of trailer

First tell your insurance company, and ensure that the car and trailer combination will be properly insured.

The regulations governing towing and trailers are complex and have changed recently to meet EC requirements. This is a summary only: if you plan to tow a sizeable trailer it's essential that you obtain expert advice.

Commercial, moi?

If you're a private car driver you doubtless reckon not – and hope not, since commercial driving is subject to regulations including the use of tachographs. But be wary: the courts have held that towing a horse box containing a pony from a gymkhana where it won prize money counted as commercial transport.

How much weight can you tow?

As a general rule the Maximum Towing Capacity (MTC) of vehicles is their own weight (that is, a car weighing 1200 Kg (approx. 1.18 tons) can tow a trailer of up to 1200 Kg provided the trailer is fitted with brakes. However it may be unwise to approach this limit, especially if you're towing something such as a caravan which has a high volume for its mass. The Caravan Club's recommendation is that the weight of this type of trailer should not exceed 85% of the weight of the towing vehicle.

By law, a vehicle can only tow an unbraked trailer of up to 50% of its own weight or 750 Kg (approx. 0.74 tons), whichever is less.

Off-road 4-wheel drive vehicles have a greater towing capacity, up to 150% of their own weight.

It's also important to consider the combined effect of the load in the car itself and the load of the trailer. The Maximum Authorised Mass (MAM) of a vehicle is the maximum that it's authorised to weigh – including the weight of its passengers and load. Both towing vehicles and trailers have MAMs. The Gross Train Weight (GTW) is the maximum weight a vehicle can handle safely, in terms of being able to brake effectively and find the power to go up steep hills. The GTW consists of the weight of the vehicle itself (including all its load) and the weight of any trailers towed (including their load). A car loaded up to its MAM with a full complement of passengers, a boot full of luggage, a roof rack and a cycle carrier may not have the GTW to carry a trailer of its maximum towing capacity.

Light trailers fitted with brakes can legally operate at MAMs up to 3500 Kg (approx. 3.44 tons). They mustn't be more than 2.3 m (5.5 ft) wide, although the load can overhang this width by up to 0.3 m (1 ft) on each side if it's adequately marked and lit. Their maximum permissible length is 7.0 m (23 ft), excluding the drawbar.

Tow bars

In general, the tow bar fitted to a car should be compatible with the car. EC regulations now restrict newer models of car (new designs – rather than mere facelifts – first sold after 1st January 1996, and all cars first sold after 1st January 1998) to using accessories that have been type approved. It's also important to ensure that the tow bar and trailer have compatible couplings and coupling heights. And all tow bars must have a 7-pin socket (more than one, if the trailer has greater electrical requirements than exterior lighting) so that the trailer's road lights can be connected.

Be very cautious if you use tow bar-mounted accessories – for example, a cycle rack or drop plates. They can cause additional weight and stability problems.

Lights and indicators

It's a legal requirement that the car driver be aware of the adequate operation of the trailer's indicators. A tell-tale flashing light or a buzzer in the car can achieve this.

It's also a legal requirement that a car's rear lights and number plate be clearly visible at all times. It's important to ensure that rear loads, including cycle racks, don't obscure them. If they are obstructed, there should be a lighting board (not a trailer board, which has red reflective triangles, and is also required behind a trailer) fitted behind the load or trailer to replicate the lights and number plate.

Trailers should have white front marker lights and amber side marker lights (older trailers can have white forward-facing and red rear-facing lights). The lights need to indicate adequately the size of the trailer and load, and if the load overhangs it may be necessary to use additional lights and/or reflective marker boards.

Towing broken down cars on A-Frames and towing dollies

Don't. It's illegal, unless they are towed by specialist recovery vehicles. Neither A-frames nor towing dollies have effective braking on all wheels, and with the weight of the towed car they will exceed the permissible weight for unbraked trailers.

Brakes on trailers

Must be fitted to all wheels. The current requirement is for Hydraulically Damped Auto-Reverse brakes, which are very efficient when the trailer is moving forwards and also allow it to be reversed easily. The trailer also needs a parking brake which will keep it still on a slope of up to 1 in 6 (18%).

Wheels and tyres

Trailers frequently use specialist wheels and tyres. Because spares may not be easy to buy in an emergency, it's a good idea to carry one. Their tyres may look like the tyres on cars, but because the load is often heavier, they may have a higher-ply construction and wheel rims of thicker steel. The inflation pressures are often high compared to car tyres, perhaps 90 psi. It's important to follow the manufacturer's instructions.

Driving in snowy and icy conditions

The best advice is – stay at home if you can.

- Clear any snow off your car thoroughly before you set out, paying particular attention to the windows. If your windows mist up when you get in the car, wait until the demister has cleared them before setting off.

- If the visibility has fallen, used dipped headlights.

- Maintain a good gap between your own car and the vehicle in front.

- Drive slowly, and brake gently. Try to avoid braking and steering at the same time. Give yourself plenty of time when you need to slow down or stop, since stopping distances may be ten times what they are in good conditions.

- Occasionally test your brakes very gently. They may be affected if snow becomes packed around the front wheels or the underside of the car.

- If you drive regularly in bad conditions, consider fitting snow chains, or M&S (mud and snow) tyres which have a specially designed tread pattern to help them maintain a good grip.

- Road markings may be invisible under the snow. Be cautious. If you're not certain the priority is yours, then stop.

Driving in fog

- Clean your windscreen before setting out: you need all the visibility you can muster.

- If you can't see clearly, use dipped headlights. Use front fog lights (if you have them) and/or rear fog lights if the visibility is seriously reduced. Remember to switch them off when visibility improves. You may find that the full beam of your headlamps (necessary if you're to use your front fog lights) simply reflects back off the fog, and dipped lights give you better overall visibility. Try alternating between fog lights and dipped beams.

- Use your windscreen wipers and demisters. A rear window heater may also aid visibility.

- Keep a safe distance from the vehicle in front, and don't hang on to its tail lights. In thick fog, if you can see the vehicle in front you're probably too close to it, unless you're travelling very slowly. Hugging its tail lights is dangerous, and may give you a false sense of security. If a vehicle hugs your bumper, avoid the temptation to accelerate away.

- Drive slowly. You should always be able to pull up within the distance you can see clearly. Check your speed regularly since it can be deceptive in poor visibility.

- When you slow down, use your brakes early, so that your brake lights warn drivers behind you.

- When the word 'Fog' is shown on a roadside signal but the road ahead appears to be clear, be prepared for a bank of fog or drifting smoke ahead. Fog can drift rapidly and is often patchy.

- The road surface is often slippery in fog. Your stopping distance will be increased accordingly.

- When you come to a junction in thick fog, it's a good idea to turn off the stereo and open the windows so you can listen for other cars: you may be able to hear them before you can see them. When stationary, keep your foot on the brake pedal so your brake lights will warn other drivers. Don't hesitate to use your horn.

- Try to avoid parking on the road in fog: other cars will come across you suddenly, which could be dangerous. Find an off-street parking place if at all possible.

- If you break down, make every effort to get your car off the road. If that's impossible, use your sidelights and your hazard lights to warn other drivers that you're there. Never leave your car parked or broken-down on the wrong side of the road.

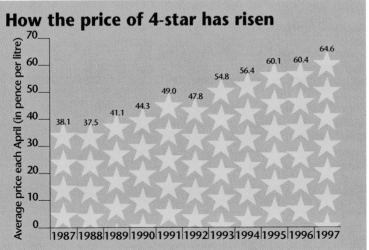

How the price of 4-star has risen

Average price each April (in pence per litre)

1987	1988	1989	1990	1991	1992	1993	1994	1995	1996	1997
38.1	37.5	41.1	44.3	49.0	47.8	54.8	56.4	60.1	60.4	64.6

They're caused by your tyres losing their grip on the road. This usually happens when you alter speed or direction, or drive up or down hill. It's more likely to happen if the road is particularly slippery (with water, ice, packed snow and frost, wet mud or leaves, or a generally loose surface) and if your tyres have a shallow tread pattern and therefore a less than ideal grip.

Harsh or uncontrolled braking often causes skids, because it shifts the car's weight towards the front wheels. The rear wheels readily lock as a result. If you don't ease up on the brakes, the front wheels may lock as well.

How to avoid skids

Keep your speed down when you drive in slippery conditions. Ensure that your brakes and tyres are well maintained and generally in good condition. Try to accelerate or brake in a steady and controlled manner. When you need to change direction, execute the manoeuvre steadily and smoothly.

When a skid happens

If you're braking, release the brake pedal to allow the wheels to turn. Then brake again more gently. Repeat the release-brake sequence as often as necessary: this is known as 'cadence braking'. Anti-lock braking systems (ABS) apply cadence braking automatically, so there's no need to do this in a car with ABS.

Turn the steering wheel in the same direction as the skid: if the rear of the car is swinging left, you should steer to the left. Try not to over-correct.

If it's the front rather than the back wheels that are sliding, release the accelerator and/or brake. Wait until the wheels regain some grip before trying to steer.

Snaking

A trailer 'snaking' (swinging from side to side) behind a towing vehicle is caused by instability in the pairing. Various problems could cause this. It's worth checking:

- the security of the tow bar.

- the coupling height.

- the nose weight.

- tyre pressures on both car and trailer.

- and the distribution of the trailer load.

Driving fast makes the snaking worse

If your trailer starts to snake, take your feet off both pedals. Hold the steering wheel straight. Don't steer into the snake, it will only make it worse.

The green driver

The first rule for a green driver is, don't drive unless you need to. Consider whether an alternative form of transport might be appropriate. Walking and cycling can save you time over short distances (and even over quite long distances in Inner London). Short journeys are bad for your car, particularly if it's a newer model with a catalytic converter, so you'll also be looking after your car.

For longer journeys, consider using public transport.

Whatever your journey, take a few minutes to plan your route carefully before you begin. Driving excess miles because you've taken a wrong turning or chosen an indirect route is expensive and frustrating for you, and bad for the environment.

A bike in London saves you time

For journeys in Inner London, a bike is typically faster than a car. A 1994 survey showed that journeys which took on average 22 minutes by car took only 18 minutes by bike. Journeys which took 50 minutes by car took 48 minutes by bike.

Tune your engine

and have your car serviced regularly. A properly tuned engine will burn no more fuel than is necessary, thus preserving natural resources, and will emit the lowest possible amount of hydrocarbons and carbon monoxide.

The catalytic converter

All new cars have been required to use catalytic converters since January 1993. Catalytic converters dramatically reduce the emission level from the exhaust, and contribute to a cleaner atmosphere. MOT regulations for car emissions are much tighter for new cars, and from 1st January 1997 an EC directive reduced the allowable emissions for new cars still further.

Catalytic converters are fragile, and expensive to replace. If your car is equipped with a cat, be careful not to bump it hard over rough ground or sleeping policemen, and not to hit the exhaust end-pipe against a wall or kerb. Never fill the tank with leaded petrol which will make the cat useless. Avoid bump-starting the car, since the unburned fuel released will contaminate the cat. (It's okay however, in case of starting problems, to jump-start it from another car's battery.)

Is a diesel car better?

In environmental terms, yes, particularly if your journeys are mostly long ones. A diesel vehicle on average travels 30% farther on a fixed amount of fuel than a petrol vehicle.

Keep an eye on those smoky lorries

If you run across commercial diesel vehicles with excessively smoky exhausts, it's worth reporting them to ensure that the fault is rectified. The Vehicle Inspectorate runs a Smoky Vehicle Hotline. Phone your local VI office, and given them all the details you can of the registration number, the type of vehicle, when and where you saw it, and if possible the name of the firm operating it.

Avoid town centres

Most major towns and cities now have park and ride schemes which enable you to park on the edge and take the bus into the centre. They're more economical then finding a city-centre parking space, they're better for the environment, and when combined with bus priority measures they give you a faster journey too.

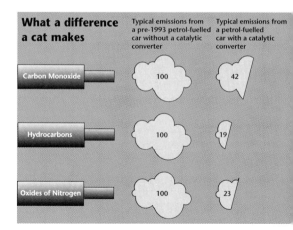

What a difference a cat makes	Typical emissions from a pre-1993 petrol-fuelled car without a catalytic converter	Typical emissions from a petrol-fuelled car with a catalytic converter
Carbon Monoxide	100	42
Hydrocarbons	100	19
Oxides of Nitrogen	100	23

How to use less fuel

- Plan all your trips carefully in advance, to ensure you cover no more distance than is necessary.

- Carry nothing more than you need to. That box of junk you forgot to take out of the boot is adding to the car's weight and increasing its fuel requirements.

- Remove the roof rack when you've finished using it. The drag it creates makes your car less aerodynamic and more fuel-hungry.

- Park so as to drive off forwards. You're making additional demands of the engine if you reverse when it's cold.

- When you start the engine, turn off the demisters, the windscreen heater, the radio, the lights. That'll help the car to start as rapidly as possible. Switch on the devices you really need once the engine's running.

- Be sparing with open windows and sunroofs. Let enough fresh air in to keep yourself alert, but open windows affect the car's aerodynamics and increase its fuel consumption.

- Keep your speed steady, and don't drive faster than you really need to. Increase your speed and you're increasing your fuel consumption. Don't accelerate too harshly, and try to minimise your braking by easing your foot off the accelerator in good time.

- In an automatic, when you pause for more than a second or two (at a red light, for instance) select 'N'.

- Use the highest possible gear for the speed you travel at. Lower gears increase your petrol consumption.

- Check your tyre pressures regularly. You'll use more fuel if you drive with under-inflated tyres.

Driving **abroad**

Documents and regulations

Documentation

Your UK driving licence will be valid for a stay of up to six months in most countries, provided you're over the minimum driving age (in most countries, 18). Especially if you're travelling to a country that doesn't use the Roman alphabet, a translation could be useful.

An International Driving Permit (obtainable through motoring organisations) is advisable if you're travelling outside Europe.

Your insurance may not be valid (or may be restricted) if you travel abroad. If in any doubt, consult your broker or insurer before your trip. A Green Card (International Motor Insurance Certificate) is normally required in European countries outside the EC, and is an useful proof of insurance in EC countries. If you're taking your car outside Europe, consult your insurer.

It's important to take your V5 Vehicle Registration Document (never leave it in your car) as proof that you're entitled to drive the car. If you're using a hired or leased car, the hirer or leaser should provide you with a Hired/Leased Vehicle Certificate. In virtually all countries you will need a GB sticker. In Spain, it's advisable to have a Bail Bond, which will help you keep out of jail in the event of an accident. Your insurer or motoring organisation can advise you.

Between some countries it is useful to have an E card (displayed on your windscreen) which helps you cross borders without delay. Of course you'll also need to check your general documentation, including your passport and health/travel insurance.

Driving regulations

All countries have slightly different driving regulations, including speed limits. It's important to be aware of the regulations before driving in a foreign country. The charts on pages 76 and 77 provide basic information as at the time of going to press, but you should check on any changes (your motoring organisation can advise you, or consult the country's local tourist office) before travelling.

In particular:

- In most countries it's compulsory to wear seat belts in the front seats. In most it's compulsory to wear them if fitted in rear seats, and in some it's compulsory to have them fitted. Suitable child restraints are also commonly required.

- Many countries have regulations limiting the age of front-seat passengers. If you're driving with children, it's safest for them to travel in the rear seats.

- In many countries, buses and trams have priority over cars. Priorities at junctions and roundabouts may also be different from those in the UK. Priority to vehicles on the right (e.g. coming on to a roundabout in a right-hand drive country) is common. In Canada and the US it's often permissible to turn right at red traffic lights if the way is clear.

- Most countries have drink/driving limits, and in some it's not permissible to drink and drive at all. The best advice is always not to drink and drive.

- In many countries spot fines are levied for motoring offences. You're not allowed to continue with your journey until you've paid up. It's useful always to have some ready cash with you. Be warned though that the fines can be heavy.

- Parking regulations can be different from those in the UK. Parking may not be permissible outside marked parking spaces, even when there is no indication on the roadside. It's safest always to park in a designated car park or parking space. Never park facing away from the flow of traffic.

- In many countries tolls are charged for the use of motorways, bridges and tunnels. The tolls can amount to a sizeable sum if you're travelling a long distance. Your motoring organisation may be able to advise you on a route which suits your pocket. In some instances the tolls must be paid by credit or bank debit card. It's advisable to take one or two common cards with you. In Switzerland and some other countries it's necessary to pay a tax and obtain a permit in advance, before driving on toll roads.

Driving regulations – a round-up

This is a summary only of some of the more basic regulations. It's essential to check on the precise regulations in the countries you intend to visit before travelling.

Country	Min. driving/car hire age	Motorway speed limit	Other roads speed limit	Speed limit built-up areas	Motorway (and other) tolls	Drink-driving limit	Also note
			When not with trailer (usually lower with trailer)				
Austria	18	130 kmh	100 kmh	50 kmh	yes + mountain passes	80mg/100ml	
Belgium	18	120 kmh	90 kmh	50 kmh	none	80mg/100ml	Priority to trams
Canada	min. car hire 25	100 kmh	60/80 kmh	40 kmh	few	80mg/100ml	Headlights in daylight some provinces. Right turn on red light (ex.Quebec)
Denmark	18	110 kmh	80 kmh	50 kmh		80mg/100ml	Dipped headlights at all times
Eire	17	70 mph	40/55 mph	30 mph	no	10mg/100ml	
France	18	130 kmh	90/110 kmh	45/50 kmh	common	50mg/100ml	All speed limits less in rain or snow
Germany	18	130 kmh	100 kmh	50 kmh	no	80mg/100ml	Speed limits advisory
Greece	18	120 kmh	110 kmh	50 kmh	on two roads	50mg/100ml	No horns in town centres. Licence translation useful
Italy	18	110/130 kmh	90 kmh	50 kmh	yes	80mg/100ml	Licence translation useful. Motorway limit depends on car size
Netherlands	18	100/125 kmh	56 kmh	50 kmh	few bridges + tunnels	50mg/100ml	Priority to trams & buses
Norway	18	90 kmh	80 kmh	30/50 kmh	yes	50mg/100ml	Dipped headlights at all times
Portugal	18	120 kmh	90 kmh	50 kmh	yes	50mg/100ml	
Spain	18	125 kmh	90/100 kmh	50 kmh	yes	80mg/100ml	Bail bond advisable
Sweden	18	110 kmh	90 kmh	30/50 kmh	rare	20mg/100ml	Dipped headlights at all times
Switzerland	18	120 kmh	80 kmh	50 kmh	yes (buy sticker)	80mg/100ml	
Turkey	18	90 kmh	90 kmh	50 kmh	yes	50mg/100ml	
USA	car hire 18/21	55/65 mph	45 mph	20/30 mph	some states	50mg/100ml	Right turn at red light

What you must carry where

In many countries it's either compulsory or recommended to carry the following equipment, and wherever you travel it's wise to do so.

Warning triangle

For placing in the road behind the car in the event of an accident. The type readily available in the UK is generally acceptable. Some countries have precise regulations on where it should be placed: check with your motoring organisation or with the country's tourist office for more information.

Fire extinguisher

This should be a type suitable for use in a car (normally weighing about 1 kg/2.2lb). Keep it in a secure but easily accessible position.

First aid kit

See the suggestions on page 19 for suitable contents.

Spare bulbs

Motorists' accessory shops can supply you with a set. Check that they're suitable for the lights on your car.

	Warning triangle	Fire extinguisher	First aid kit	Spare bulbs	Other
Austria	*	R	*	*	
Belgium	*	*	R	R	
Denmark	*	R	R	R	
Eire	R	R	R	R	
France	*	R	R	R	
Germany	*	R	*	R	
Greece	*	*	*	R	
Italy	*	R	R	R	
Netherlands	*	R	R	*	
Norway	*	R	R	R	
Portugal	*	R	R	R	
Spain	*	R	R	*	fuses, spare wheel
Sweden	*	R	R	R	
Switzerland	*	R	R	R	spare glasses if worn
Turkey	R	*	*	*	tool kit

* – essential

R – recommended but not compulsory

Driving in different conditions

It really is more dangerous abroad

Rate of road deaths per 100,000 population in 1995:

Great Britain	6
Australia	11
Germany	12
Italy	12
France	15
Spain	15
USA	16
Greece	21
Portugal	29

Driving on the right
Your headlights will need adjusting so that the beam dips towards the right and not the left. Headlamp converters are widely on sale at car accessory stores. Remember to remove them as soon as you return to the UK.

If your car doesn't have an external rear view mirror on the passenger side, then have one fitted before your journey. Ask your front-seat passenger (if you have one) to check visually for blind spots before you overtake.

If you have an accident
In many countries you have a legal obligation to inform the police if you have an accident.

Your insurer may issue you with an Agreed Statement of Facts form to complete. It's quite likely that the other driver involved (if there is one) will also wish to complete a form, and have you sign it. Don't refuse to sign if you're unable to translate the form – it may be against the law to do so – but do mark clearly (in English if you wish) that your signature is not an admission of liability.

Hiring a car abroad

Taking your car abroad is an expensive business, and especially if you're going some distance, you may find it's cheaper to hire a car once you arrive. Alternatively, it might be cheapest to dispense with a car of your own and simply use taxis when you need them.

The major multinational car hire firms have high overheads and correspondingly high hire charges. Their cars are generally new and reliable, however, and you may feel the extra payment is worthwhile.

If you're travelling abroad on a package deal, you may well find that the car hire you're offered as part of the package is cheaper than any arrangements you can make after your arrival.

If you're looking for a budget deal, ask locally. Avoid asking in an expensive hotel: try the café down the road, or ask at a tourist information office.

Many car hire deals include optional insurance coverage. Check carefully before committing yourself to expensive coverage. It may be that your normal insurance, or the travel insurance you've taken out, provides the necessary cover.

Be wary of deals that impose a mileage charge. Distances in some countries are very large, and the cost can mount up alarmingly.

Finally, check carefully the conditions of hire to ensure they match your requirements, especially if you plan to drive in areas without made-up roads, or to cross borders during your journey. (Both of these are forbidden by some firms.)

Driving in difficult conditions

In remote areas it may not be easy to obtain the fuel you require, and if your car runs on leaded fuel you will find it increasingly difficult to obtain in many European countries. Make sure you have plenty of fuel for each trip before you set out.

In many countries the roads in rural areas are unmade and of poor quality. Drive slowly, and ensure that your tyres and brakes are in good enough condition to cope.

In hot weather, it's important to check the coolant level regularly. If the engine begins to overheat, stop and allow it to cool down. Be wary of sunburn: cover up before you burn.

In snowy conditions it's desirable, and in some places legally necessary, to use snow tyres, studded tyres or snow chains. Check on the requirements before making your journey.

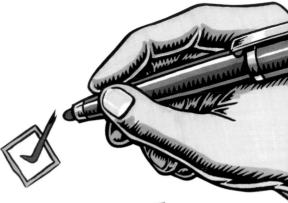

Before you set out: summary of things to remember

- [ ] Have your car serviced if you're making a long trip or travelling far from home, or if servicing and spares for your car are likely to be expensive abroad. It may be useful to carry some basic spare parts (e.g. fan belt, hoses, valves, spark plugs) with you.

- [ ] Check on the motoring regulations for each of the countries you plan to visit. Obtain any compulsory items such as a warning triangle, a spare set of bulbs and a first aid kit.

- [ ] Check your documentation and arrange any additional car insurance you need.

- [ ] Extend your breakdown coverage, if it doesn't already cover the countries you plan to visit. Your breakdown insurer/motoring organisation may also assist with planning your route.

- [ ] Arrange any medical insurance you need for the trip.

- [ ] Make arrangements to have pets cared for, plants watered and daily deliveries cancelled.

- [ ] Ensure that you will have adequate funds in the shape of cash, credit or travellers' cheques.

- [ ] Ensure that you and your car are properly equipped for the conditions you expect to encounter.

Accidents

Accident trends

Is your car relatively safe?

Drivers are more likely to be injured in a collision if they are in a small car than in a larger car. A small car hitting a large car will suffer more damage (and its occupants worse injury) than a small car hitting another small car.

But some small cars are safer than others, and so are some large cars. Research carried out from 1989 to 1994 suggested that the safest cars in each class were:

- Small cars
  Peugeot 205, Renault Clio

- Small to medium cars
  VW Golf, Volvo 300

- Medium cars
  Mercedes 190, VW Passat

- Large cars
  Volvo 700, Volvo 900

Death and Disaster – How Often it Happens

Number of accidents in which there were serious or fatal injuries in the UK:

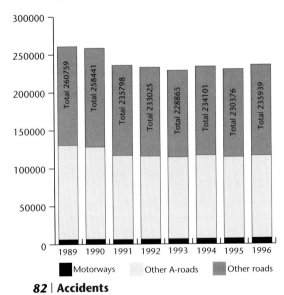

| | Motorways | Other A-roads | Other roads |

Speeding

Driving too fast has been estimated to cause 77,000 injuries and around 1,000 deaths in the UK each year.

The difference speed makes
Of course you'll brake if you realise you're likely to hit a pedestrian, bike or another vehicle. But the faster you're going, the longer your stopping distance will be (see page 50) and the greater the speed you'll still be doing at the point of collision.

- If you hit a pedestrian when you're doing 20 mph you have a 1 in 20 chance of killing them. You have a good chance of injuring them only a little if at all.

- If you hit a pedestrian when you're doing 30 mph you have

almost a 50% chance of killing them – and those who survive are likely to be seriously injured.

- If you hit a pedestrian when you're doing 40 mph you're almost certain to kill them.

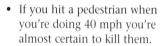

How many drivers break the speed limit
Proportion of drivers exceeding the speed limit (on uncongested roads) in 1994 research:

- Motorways   47%

- Dual carriageways
  (60 mph limit)   40%

- Single carriageways
  (60 mph limit)   10%

Dangerous situations and places

The manoeuvres

It's estimated that more than 90% of accidents are caused by a driver or rider making a mistake. These are the manoeuvres that caused car drivers to have reported accidents in 1996.

Reversing	3,921
When parked	12,566
Waiting to proceed but held up	29,712
Stopping	14,906
Starting	4,248
Doing a U-turn	2,240
Turning left (or waiting to turn)	12,253
Turning right (or waiting to turn)	43,846
Changing lane	4,142
Overtaking a moving or stationary vehicle	13,310
On a bend	28,377
Going ahead other	161,247

The locations

These are the road configurations where car drivers had reported accidents in 1996.

At a roundabout	26,052
At a T or staggered junction	107,838
At a Y junction	4,754
At a crossroads	38,557
At a multiple junction	4,691
On a slip road	4,863
At another junction	7,173
Using a private drive or entrance	15,831
More than 20 metres from any junction	121,106

Keep your speed down

Remember the legal speed limit is an upper limit. In poor conditions you should keep well under it.

Hints to help you avoid accidents

- Drive particularly carefully near airports and ferry ports. You can expect to find a higher proportion of drivers unfamiliar with the roads, and of tired and hurried drivers.

- Never accept a lift from a driver who has been drinking, is under the influence of drugs or medication, or who otherwise seems in an unfit state to drive.

- Drive particularly carefully when following learners (not all tuition cars have dual controls) and probationers with 'P' plates.

- Stow all luggage carefully. Be particularly careful putting items on the front passenger seat: they might slip and obstruct the pedals or gear stick.

- Have your eyesight tested regularly.

- Stop regularly during long journeys – at least every two hours – and more frequently if you feel tired or inattentive.

- Use your indicators every single time you change direction.

- Try to avoid passing schools when pupils are arriving or leaving. If you must, then drive carefully.

- If it's snowing or foggy, make your journey only if it's essential. Over 48% of car accidents in snow involve cars skidding.

- Never drink and drive. Even one drink will impair your driving ability.

- Ensure all passengers wear seatbelts. Whenever possible, children should travel in the rear seats.

- Check your tyres and brakes regularly.

Keeping your car secure

Whenever you leave your car:

- close the windows completely, unless there are children or pets in the car. (If you're leaving the car for more than a few moments, take them with you.)

- lower the radio aerial to prevent vandalism.

- remove the ignition key, even if you're only paying for petrol or parking in your drive.

- engage the steering lock.

- use a security device (see below) if you have one.

- lock the car and remove the key, however briefly you're leaving the car.

- take all movable contents (including the stereo and mobile phone) with you, or if that's not possible, lock them in the boot.

Mark the stereo and other valuable equipment permanently with the car registration number, particularly if they're removable in one piece.

Use your garage if you have one. Your car's much safer there than on the road.

A quarter of all recorded car crime happens in car parks. Choose a well lit, well supervised park with limited entry and exit points. Avoid dark corners. Park within sight of the attendant if there is one.

An increasing amount of crime happens on the road. Keep purses and wallets out of sight, and don't leave bags or briefcases on the seat by an open window.

Security features

Many new cars have security features such as immobilisers, central locking, lockable fuel caps and electronic locks as standard equipment. Check what's provided before you buy.

If your car's older, try using a steering wheel or gear stick lock. They're cheap but effective. Electronic immobilisers and alarms are good but expensive. It's also worthwhile having the registration number etched into windows.

Electronic tracking systems such as the AA-supported TRACKER tag your car with a hidden homing device, so the police can locate it if it's stolen. For high value cars they're a worthwhile investment.

Motoring
offences

The penalty you pay

There are over 1000 motoring offences, but many of them are quite obscure and a handful of them account for the vast majority of fines and prosecutions.

Parliament sets the maximum penalties for road traffic offences. For offences that are tried in court (that is, not fixed-penalty offences) the courts decide on the precise penalty to be imposed. See pages 16-17 for more information.

Of course the fine, penalty points, disqualification or prison sentence that the courts may impose is not your only punishment if you commit a motoring offence. There may well be a negative effect on your social life or on your career. You'll almost certainly find you have to pay more for car insurance in future. And if you're at fault in an accident in which someone is seriously injured or dies, you'll have to live with that knowledge for the rest of your life.

If you are summonsed on a serious motoring offence, you should obtain expert legal advice. This brief summary of the possible penalties is intended only to provide an indication of what could happen.

The Vehicle Defect Rectification Scheme

This scheme was designed to ensure that drivers stopped by the police have to correct relatively minor car defects, without the police needing to go through the procedure of charging them with a motoring offence.

Under the scheme, if a police officer checks your car and finds a defect, s/he issues you with a VDRS Notice. (The forms used vary from one police force to another.) You're then obliged to have the defects repaired, and to take the car to an MOT testing station which checks that the repairs have been carried out. Once the MOT tester has signed the form, you send it in to the police. There's no fine to pay, but obviously you have to bear the expense of the repairs and to pay a testing fee.

Categories of offence and penalties

These are common non-endorsable fixed penalty offences – in other words you'll be punished by a fine, not by points on your driving licence:

- Exhaust emission offences.
- Failure to provide details of the vehicle ownership or driver.
- Lighting offences.
- Most (non-dangerous) parking offences.
- Not notifying a change of vehicle ownership.
- Seat belt offences.
- Stopping on a Clearway.
- Stopping on a motorway hard shoulder.

These are offences which can be dealt with by a fixed penalty notice, but the penalty can include an endorsement:

- Defective tyres.
- Driving not in accordance with a driving licence.
- Failure to comply with traffic lights.
- Failure to comply with police/traffic signs.
- Leaving a vehicle in a dangerous position.
- Pedestrian crossing offences.
- Speeding.
- Using the vehicle in a dangerous condition.

For any offence which carries penalty points the courts have a discretionary power to order a period of disqualification. (This won't happen, of course, if you accept a fixed penalty and don't ask for the case to be heard in court.)

These offences are not dealt with by a fixed penalty, and may result in disqualification:

- Being in charge of a vehicle with excess alcohol.
- Driving in the wrong direction on a motorway.
- Doing a U-turn on a motorway.
- Failure to report an accident.
- Failure to stop after an accident.
- Refusing to give a specimen after being in charge of a vehicle.
- Speeding at more than 25 mph over the speed limit.
- Taking a vehicle without consent.

Amassing 12 or more penalty points within a 3-year period.
This is known as the totting-up procedure. Normally you will receive at least 6 months' disqualification, and longer for a second or subsequent offence.

Serious offences

You can expect to be disqualified for at least 12 months for these more serious offences:

- Aggravated taking a vehicle without consent.

- Causing death by careless driving while under the influence of drink or drugs.

- Causing death by dangerous driving.

- Dangerous driving.

- Driving with excess alcohol.

- Manslaughter involving a motor vehicle.

If you're convicted for a second time within ten years of drink-driving (or being in charge of a car with excess alcohol) then you can expect to be disqualified for at least three years, even if you managed to avoid disqualification for the first offence.

Finally, the courts have the power to send you to prison for the following offences:

- Aggravated taking a vehicle without consent.

- Being in charge of a car with excess alcohol.

- Causing danger to road users.

- Causing death by careless driving while under the influence of drink or drugs.

- Causing death by dangerous driving.

- Dangerous driving.

- Driving with excess alcohol.

- Driving while disqualified.

- Failure to report an accident.

- Failure to stop after an accident.

- Manslaughter involving a motor vehicle.

- Refusing to provide a specimen after being in charge of a car.

- Refusing to provide a specimen after driving.

- Taking a vehicle without consent.

Drivers convicted of drinking and driving twice within 10 years, or once if they are over 2½ times the legal limit, or those who refuse to give a specimen, also have to satisfy the DVLA's Medical Branch that they don't have an alcohol problem and are otherwise fit to drive before their licence is returned at the end of their period of disqualification.

Probation for new drivers

On 1st June 1997 the penalties have been changed for drivers in the first two years after passing their first test. Penalty points are given for driving offences in the usual way, but if the driver tots up more than six points in the two years (including any pre-test points that haven't expired, and points for any offence committed but not sentenced within the two years) then his or her licence is revoked. S/he has to apply for a new provisional licence and take the driving test (including the theory test) all over again.

Normally only the standard test is taken, but if the courts order an extended test to be taken, then this is taken instead.

This process can only happen once, but the points aren't removed by the revocation, and a driver who commits another offence after regaining his/her licence could be disqualified.

Drinking and driving

The legal limit for drinking and driving is measured as:

- a breath alcohol level of 35 mg/100 ml

- or a blood alcohol level of 80 mg/100 ml

- or an urine level of 107 mg/100 ml.

The amount of alcohol's equivalent in each case: these are just different ways of testing for it.

However it's not wise to think of this as a safe limit. Although you won't be prosecuted for drink-driving if your alcohol intake is below this limit, your driving could still suffer.

How much is the limit in terms of drinks?

It varies depending on the size of the drink and the strength of it, and on the constitution of the person drinking. As an example, an average-sized man could be over the limit by drinking as little as two pints of ordinary strength bitter. An average woman could be over the limit after drinking one pint of ordinary bitter. If for example you're run down, coming down with a cold, or haven't eaten much recently, you may find you're over the limit even sooner.

Half a pint of beer contains roughly as much alcohol as a 125 ml glass of wine, a 50 ml pub measure of port or sherry, or a 25 ml pub measure of spirits. Spirit measures in Scotland and Northern Ireland are larger, and at home you're likely to pour more generous measures.

Drink-Drive Facts

- At twice the legal limit you're more than 50 times more likely to be involved in a fatal accident.

- Up to 19% of all drivers and motorcycle riders killed are above the legal limit.

- At night between 10 pm and 4 am, around 50% of those killed are above the limit.

- In 1996, 781,000 people were asked to take a roadside breath test. 101,000 (13%) either tested positive or refused.

- Drink drive accidents happen on short journeys, 70% of them within 3 miles of setting out.

- In 1979, 51% of adults questioned admitted drinking and driving on at least one occasion in the previous week. In 1995 this had fallen to 25%.

The impact on your driving

After drinking alcohol:

- your co-ordination is less.

- your reactions are slower.

- your judgement of speed, distance and risk is affected.

- you may have a false sense of confidence.

Once you reach the legal limit your driving will almost certainly be erratic. Your vision may be impaired, and you may not notice cars, cyclists and pedestrians until it's too late.

Getting over that drink

There's no way to get yourself quickly under the limit. Drinking coffee and water don't achieve it. Nor does a shower. Having a meal with your drink will affect the speed at which the alcohol is absorbed, but it won't stop you being affected by it.

You may still be unfit to drive in the evening after drinking at lunchtime, or in the morning after drinking the previous evening. If you drank a great deal, it may take a full day before all the alcohol has been eliminated from your system.

What drivers were caught for

These totals (all figures in thousands) include guilty verdicts in court, fixed penalty notices and written warnings for 1995.

Accident offences (e.g. failure to stop)	23
Dangerous, careless or drunken driving	189
Licence, insurance & record keeping offences	874
Neglect of traffic signs and directions and pedestrian rights	272
Speed limit offences	680
Unauthorised taking/theft of vehicle	41
Vehicle testing & condition	313
Other offences not including obstruction, waiting & parking offences	278
All offences (excluding obstruction, waiting and parking)	2670
Obstruction, waiting and parking	2290
Grand total	4960

Buying and selling a car

Choosing a car

What kind of car?
Before you consider particular models, ask yourself what type of car you need.

- What's the upper limit of your budget?

- Do you drive mainly short journeys in town? You'll be looking for a nippy car, probably petrol-driven (diesels are less suited to frequent short journeys) with a small turning circle.

- Do you drive mainly long distances on motorways? Comfort will be a priority, and you may want to opt for a more powerful car. Diesels come into their own for this type of motoring.

- What's your overall likely annual mileage?

- Do you regularly carry passengers, awkward-shaped equipment, animals? How many seats should there be, and would you prefer them to be removable? How many doors do you require? Do you need an estate or hatchback?

- Do you plan to tow a caravan or trailer? (Basic advice is on pages 62 to 64.)

- Are you or your regular passengers unusually tall/short/plump, or disabled in any way? If so, you'll need a car that meets your/their needs – for example, plenty of headroom for the driver, flexible seat adjustments, or a low sill to help you get in and out easily.

- What's your insurance status? New or young drivers, those in high risk categories, and drivers with past claims experience, may find the premiums prohibitive for expensive or fast cars.

- Do you prefer manual gears or an automatic?

New or used?
A new car is a known quantity, while there's a limited amount even the most dedicated investigator can discover about an used car. The new car should come with a warranty from the manufacturer. It'll be the latest model, and you'll benefit from developments in fuel consumption and safety/security features.

However, you'll pay for the privilege. The sharpest period of depreciation in a car is over the first few months. (In part this is false depreciation, on the list price when many cars are sold at a substantial discount. However, as a private buyer you won't rate a discount on the level of a fleet buyer or car hire organisation.)

Unsold models from the previous year often sell more cheaply than the models that supersede them. And it's often possible to find bargains in 'nearly new', 'cancelled order', 'repossession', 'ex-demonstration' or 'pre-registered' cars, with small mileages but substantial discounts off the list price.

With an used car, you need to take additional care in checking out both the car and the seller, especially if you're buying privately. Advantages however are that the depreciation will be much less steep, and that the initial faults on the car will have been ironed out by the time you buy it. If you're buying a car several years old, however, it may have had time to develop plenty more faults!

More advice on buying used cars is on pages 98 to 101.

Narrowing down the choice
Your next step will be to decide on the models that would suit you. You'll find motoring magazines (both the weekly/monthly glossies, and the specialised used car guides) an useful source of information on both new and used cars. Factors you should consider include:

- The likely purchase price, for the model and age of car you're considering.

- The resale value, with a particular eye to the length of time you plan to keep the car.

- Annual insurance costs. Some magazines indicate the insurance category of the model, and your broker can advise you what that will mean in terms of premium to you.

- Maintenance costs, including recommended service intervals and the availability of parts. Finding out, say, the cost of a 6000 mile service, a new exhaust and a set of new tyres will give you a good indication.

- Fuel consumption (and type of fuel required).

- The location of the nearest authorised dealer.

When to buy
Peak times for new cars have been January and August, but this pattern may change if the Government alters the system for allocating registration plate prefixes.

These can also be good periods for used cars, as you'll have a good choice of trade-in models. But in winter the demand is lowest, and you may find a dealer able to devote more time and trouble to assisting you.

Where to buy a used car

From a dealer

If you buy the car from a dealer you're protected by the Sale and Supply of Goods Act 1994 (and earlier Sale of Goods Acts). This adds up to a guarantee that the car is fit for its purpose, of satisfactory quality, and that statements made about it are true and accurate. You'll pay a little more than you would if you were buying from a private seller or at auction, but you may feel it's worthwhile to have this security.

Many dealers offer warranties on used cars. Your judgement of the value of the warranty will depend at least in part on your judgement of the dealer itself. Is it a reputable firm that's still likely to be in business when you need to claim under the warranty?

Specialist second-hand car dealers tend to have the widest choice of models, but you may find a better bargain if you pick up from an authorised new-car dealer a car that has been accepted in part exchange.

Most dealers advertise widely, and a local 'auto trader' magazine is an useful first port of call.

From a private seller

Prices are lower from private sellers, but this reflects the fact that when you buy privately, you have less protection than when you buy through the trade.

The seller's verbal and/or written description of the car must be accurate, and you have a legal case if you find that it isn't. If you buy from an ad, keep a copy of it in your files: it's your proof of the seller's description. A private seller must also guarantee roadworthiness in terms of the Road Traffic Acts. And if it's old enough to need one, the car should have an MOT.

Some less scrupulous dealers masquerade as private sellers, in an attempt to avoid their full liability and to persuade you that you're getting a better bargain. When you phone a private seller, it's worth asking after 'the car' rather than quoting the details in the ad. If the reply is, 'Which car?' then be wary.

It's also important to ensure that you know the seller's address, so you can contact them if you do run into difficulties. Ask to meet them and look over the car at their home; don't let them bring it to yours. Try to ensure you go into the house: it's not unknown for sellers to do business in the street outside someone else's house. Be cautious too if the phone number given belongs to a mobile.

At an auction

An auction is not for the faint-hearted, but you'll get a good price if you feel confident of buying this way.

The protection you have on a car bought at auction depends on the terms of sale. The safest cars to go for are those 'sold all good'. These should come with a guarantee on the major mechanical components, a full service history and a mileage warranty. You should be able to take an after-sale test drive on this class of car – which will generally be less than five years old – and take immediate action if it throws up any problems.

'Sold as seen' cars are generally older cars, and they come without any mechanical warranty. A visual inspection before you buy may give you some reassurance, but it's impossible even for an expert to pick up many faults which would be expensive to correct. Many would argue that these are best left to the trade, who can carry the risk of a proportion of 'rogue' cars.

Does the seller own the car?

A registration document – though essential – is not legal proof that the named keeper owns the car, and does not give any details of outstanding hire purchase or lease obligations. If you're buying second-hand it's worth paying for a check which will confirm whether the seller has a clean title to the car.

HPI is the best-known of the organisations who provide this service – originally to the trade, but now to private buyers as well. Significant information to make a buyer beware turns up for one in every three vehicles they check.

Ex-company cars

About one in nine cars is or has been company owned, so you're ruling out a sizeable section of the market if you're not prepared to consider company cars. Many buyers are wary of them because they generally have high mileages. This isn't always the case though, and a company car which belonged to a low-mileage executive could be an attractive buy.

Even reps' cars have their advantages. They will normally have been serviced very regularly, and much of the mileage may have been long-distance motorway driving. Eighty thousand miles on the motorway causes much less wear on the car than eighty thousand miles in five mile stop-start trips to the office and the shops.

Checking out a used car

First carry out a factual check; then a mechanical check is a wise precaution if you're buying privately.

- Look up the exact model and registration letter/date of registration in a used car price guide to get a sense of whether the price is right.

- If you're a member of a motoring organisation, they may be able to provide you with a report on performance of that model which will give useful background information. The *Which? Used Car Guide* performs a similar function.

- Check the registration document, which should show no signs of tampering. Compare the chassis and engine numbers given with those on the car itself. Note the number of previous owners, and ask whether there have been any corporate owners. You can check the identities of previous owners through the DVLA.

- Find out the mileage, and whether it is warranted. The service history (if available), roster of previous keepers, general condition of the car and wear on components like the

pedals should help you decide whether it's genuine.

- Ask about the service history. A full service history adds about 10% to the value of the car. If the seller has done d-i-y servicing, ask to see any documentation, e.g. receipts for replacement parts.

- Check the MOT certificate (if applicable) and tax disc.

- Accident damage, however well repaired, has a lasting effect on a car. Ask if the car has ever been declared a total loss. An HPI check (see page 99) should verify this information.

A check by experts
Several motoring organisations offer a car-checking service to members and sometimes to non-members. The mechanic will check the car over thoroughly and report to you on its condition.

Checking the car over yourself
Checking the regular items you check on your own car will tell you if the owner has been conscientious, at least in the recent past.

- Inspect the cooling system. Is the coolant level right? Is the liquid green or blue (indicating the presence of antifreeze)? Is it clean?

- Check the dipstick. Is the oil at the right level? Does it seem black and sludgy, or does it appear in reasonable condition?

- Check the bodywork carefully. Is there any rust? Does the colour match on all panels? Are there any wavy panels? (This could be a sign of damage mended with filler.) Any chips in the paintwork? Look around the windscreen sealing rubbers, and in the engine compartment. If the car has been damaged and resprayed there may be signs of overspray. Look in the boot, checking the spare wheel (and under) for signs of damage.

- Check the tyres. Are they at or near (or even under) the minimum tread? The car manual will tell you the recommended pressures. Check them – using a portable gauge, or at a garage during your test run.

- Switch on the ignition. (Does the car start readily?) Listen to the engine – is it ticking over regularly? Are there any rumbling or knocking noises?

- Switch on and check all lights and indicators.

- Rev the engine hard, ease off the throttle, and check (or ask a partner to check) whether there's much sign of smoke coming from the exhaust.

- Ask for a test drive. Check the brakes during your drive: are they effective? Is the car comfortable to handle, and are the gear changes smooth? A hill start will show you if there's any slippage in the clutch. Also check the dashboard instrumentation: as far as you can tell, is everything working?

Once you've bought the car

Of course you'll do the paperwork and fix the insurance straight away. Your previous insurer may not offer you the best terms on a different car: it's worth getting several quotes.

If you haven't bought through a dealer, it's also worth dropping the car into your garage. If it needs a service, have one carried out. Have the wheel alignment and balancing checked; and if there are any defective parts, have them replaced immediately.

Finally, if the car didn't come with etched windows and an anti-theft device, now's the time to improve its security.

Selling your car

Preparing to sell your car

First impressions count. Anyone who considers buying your car, whether it's a dealer accepting it in part-exchange or a private buyer responding to your small ad, will be more impressed if the car appears to be well cared for and in good condition.

A full service may not enhance its value by as much as it will cost you, but it's certainly worth:

- checking the tyres and inflating them to the correct pressure.

- checking the oil and topping up if necessary to the correct level.

- checking the coolant and the water reservoir and topping them up.

Finally, give the car a very thorough clean both inside and out. If the engine's very dirty, having that cleaned might also be worthwhile.

Assemble the paperwork

Check that the registration document, MOT certificate and road tax disc are current and in good order. If the car has been serviced regularly, assemble your proof: garage receipts, or stamps in the car's service manual. If you've maintained it yourself, it's necessary to assemble receipts and any other proof. A full service history will add up to 10% to your car's value, so it's worth taking time to do this thoroughly.

You can sell the car with its tax disc included, but you're not obliged to, and if the car's likely to go cheap you may prefer to claim a refund on the unexpired portion of the excise tax, and leave your buyer to retax the car.

How much should you ask?

Check the current edition of any good used car price guide. It'll give you an indication of what you should be asking, although the exact price will depend on the mileage and condition of the car, the route you choose to sell it, and how anxious you are for a speedy sale. Ask initially for a little more than you expect to get, as any buyer likes to haggle and feel they've got a bargain.

Selling to a dealer

Unless you're selling a particularly rare or desirable car, you'll get the best terms when selling your car through a dealer if you part-exchange it for a newer model. If that's not your intention, don't go to a franchised main dealer: try the second-hand car specialists instead.

Part-exchanging can give you a good deal if you have a moderately popular model which is in good condition, and has a reasonable mileage. You still can't expect to receive as good a price from a dealer as you would from a private sale, however: the dealer has to make a profit.

If your car is suitable for the dealer to retail second-hand (for example, if it's the same make as their dealership) you'll get better terms than if they'll need to resell it to another dealer or at auction.

Don't be seduced by a good part-exchange offer into failing to check the terms you're being offered on the replacement car you're buying. Discounts on new cars (and on used cars for cash buyers) can vary widely from dealer to dealer.

Selling privately

Again, a desirable model in good condition with moderate mileage and a full service record will sell best. If you've something less ideal to offer, this may still be the most profitable route for you. Remember though that you'll have to pay for adverts whether your car sells as a result or not.

- Check the local and national press and decide where best to advertise your car. If you're in a remote location, the local press may be your best bet: a London or Manchester buyer could be wary of making the trek to view your car. Check what the ad will cost before committing yourself.

- Describe the car clearly, using the conventions employed by other ads in the publication you choose. Ask a little more than you expect to get, to allow for haggling.

- Be honest about your car. It's fine to emphasise its good points and play down its failings, but don't be tempted to lie. Don't turn back the mileage gauge.

- Be conscious of security. Don't let anyone drive off unaccompanied for a test drive: it may be the last you ever see of your car. If your insurance won't cover the test drive, check that theirs will.

- Be wary if you're offered a deposit, particularly if it's small. You could turn down a cash buyer, only to have the deposit-giver change their mind once your ad is a distant memory. Agree clearly the terms of the deposit. If it's giving the purchaser an option on the car, it's reasonable to specify that at least a part of it's non-refundable.

- Once you have a firm offer, play fair with your buyer. Don't dump them if you get a better offer.

- Ask for payment in cash or by banker's draft. If the seller insists on a cheque, wait for it to clear before handing over the keys.

Selling at auction

Selling at auction won't get you the best return for your car, but if it's a difficult-to-shift model that you want to see the back of, it may be a worthwhile method for you to choose.

Phone the auctioneers. They'll give you information on the procedure. You normally pay a fee to enter your car in the auction, and a commission on a successful sale. It's worth setting a reserve (there may be a fee for this too) if your car is moderately valuable, or it could be sold for just a few pounds.

Motoring
organisations

Why join a motoring organisation?

Different motoring organisations have different characteristics, and offer different services. These are some of the common benefits.

Breakdown insurance
Even if your car won't start at home, it'll cost you to call out a mechanic to get it going. If you break down far from home, in a motorway or a remote place, you'll not only face a callout charge. You may also have to stump up for:

- towing fees, to get the car to a garage equipped to undertake the repairs.

- possibly accommodation in the area, if you're not able to get home as you planned.

- and possibly a hire car to get you to your appointment.

Breakdown organisations spread the risk. At the simplest, they might simply provide a tow to a garage if it's not realistic for you to make a roadside repair. At their most complex they will cover you anywhere in Europe (and beyond, in the case of specialist organisations), carrying all the additional costs you incur including accommodation, additional transport costs and even the cost of hiring a substitute driver.

This service doesn't come cheap. It's an understandable concern of breakdown insurers to avoid the bad-risk cars and drivers – old cars, drivers who don't maintain their vehicles and drivers with accident records – and a specialist organisation which weeds out these undesirable customers may offer you better terms, if you qualify for them.

Technical advice
Many motoring organisations have specialist staff who provide technical advice to members (and sometimes to non-members, at a price). This includes:

- specialist reports on particular makes and models of car, which give you guidance when you're planning to buy.

- detailed technical inspections as a precaution before you buy an used car.

- advice on particular technical problems you encounter while driving, maintaining or repairing your car.

Route planning
Some motoring organisations offer a route planning service, in the UK and/or farther afield. They will take account not only of the distance to travel, but also of aspects such as the condition of the roads, known bottlenecks and hotspots, and major roadworks. Some services allow you to specify the fastest route, a quiet route or a particularly scenic route passing through places of interest. (It's worth checking out computer programs that fulfil the same function, too.)

General motoring information
Most organisations produce regular magazines or newsletters. Particularly if you don't regularly read the motoring press, this could be very important to you.

Commercial services
Most organisations have links with commercial services, from insurance to member loans to package tours. Sometimes the volume of mail can be a problem, but you could pick up some useful bargains.

Research
As well as providing technical advice on specific queries, several of the major organisations carry out research on aspects of driving and transport generally. Though this is not of immediate practical benefit to you, you may be happy to see your subscription going to support it.

Lobbying services
Motoring organisations work on behalf of motorists – and many of them lobby the Government to ensure that motorists' interests are taken into account when new legislation is planned.

Social events
Some organisations have local branches which organise a programme of social events particularly geared towards motorists.

Driver training
Some organisations offer advanced or specialist driver training, and virtually all are sources of advice if you're looking for further training.

Which to join?
Some better-known motoring organisations are briefly profiled on the next few pages. (This is not intended as an endorsement of them, or a disparagement of those not mentioned.) They are open to all drivers, or in some cases all who meet their standard of driving. Some larger employers also have motoring clubs (the Civil Service Motoring Association is a good example) which may be more economical for those eligible to join.

The AA

for contact details see page 121

The AA was founded in 1905 to serve motorists, and today is a major organisation with over 9 million members. Breakdown services are at the core of its membership packages, but there is a very wide range of other services on offer.

The AA's services are not cheap. The lowest-level single membership, which provides roadside breakdown cover, costs £45 (£40 if you pay by direct debit) and the full-featured single membership including replacement car, overnight accommodation or help with onward travel, costs £142 (£122 by direct debit). It's worth comparing that with the likely cost if you breakdown without insurance, however.

The person not the car
Some breakdown services cover specific vehicles, but the AA's is a personal membership. If you're a member you are covered for breakdown regardless of what vehicle you're travelling in – even if you're a passenger. Joint membership and family membership are also available.

Roadside patrols
A distinctive feature of the AA's service is its roadside patrols. It has the world's largest highway patrol force, made up of trained mechanics who fix over 80% of the breakdowns they're called to at the roadside.

Other special features of the AA's breakdown coverage
The organisation holds a special register for members with special needs, to ensure they receive any necessary special treatment when they breakdown.

AA garage and hotel inspections
You're probably familiar with the AA inspection service which rates garages and hotels using a star system. Most AA-approved garages offer a discount to members.

Technical services
A full range of technical services includes Car Test reports on specific makes and models, vehicle inspections, and an Used Car Data Check which checks the car's history to discover whether it's been stolen, written-off, or there's an outstanding finance claim. The AA also offers mechanical breakdown insurance – which covers you not just against recovery costs, but also against the actual cost of repairs.

Other services

Among the other goodies on offer are:

- Full European cover – at additional cost.

- Traffic and weather information.

- A handbook and quarterly magazine (included in membership) plus many publications.

- Driver training.

- A wide range of commercial and travel services.

The RAC

for contact details see page 122

The oldest of the major motoring organisations – it's just celebrated its centenary – the RAC has been working hard recently to modernise its image, and new technology features heavily in their portfolio of services.

Personal membership

Like the AA, the RAC's is a personal membership which covers you as driver or passenger in any car. They also offer joint and family membership.

Computer-aided patrols

The RAC has its own patrols, with their movements monitored by a satellite location system. They're equipped with in-car navigation systems and use digitised Ordnance Survey maps to help them reach members quickly.

Also unique to the RAC are the patrols' CD-ROM repair manuals, designed to help the mechanics to identify and repair faults faster.

Cover options

The range begins with Individual Roadside cover, which includes roadside repairs and a tow to the nearest garage, and works up to full European cover. At £44 (£39 by direct debit) the basic cover just undercuts the AA.

A recent feature is the 'no call out discount' on Standard Cover (which includes roadside assistance, home start and assisted travel to any UK mainland destination): if you don't use the breakdown service all year you can claim £25 back. (The basic subscription is £110, or £105 by direct debit.)

RAC technical services

Like the AA, the RAC is strong on the technical side. Technical advice, technical examinations of cars you're considering buying, legal advice, and traffic information (there's a web site on http://www.rac.co.uk) are all available to members.

Green Flag

Green Flag too is big business, with over 3.5 million members. It doesn't have its own patrols, but uses a nationwide network of 1,500 independent operators and 6,000 mechanics. In case you fear that's less reliable than the own-patrol system, Green Flag gives you a £10 rebate if its mechanic doesn't reach you within an hour. 35 minutes is their quoted average callout time.

Green Flag covers the car, not the individual, so unlike the AA and RAC you won't be covered under their basic services if you're a passenger in someone else's car – although personal cover is available as an option.

The 'recovery only' service will interest those who feel they don't need a mechanic to repair a broken fanbelt or mend a puncture. It doesn't cover simple roadside repairs, but does retrieve your car if you have a more serious breakdown. (The mechanic judges: if s/he can repair the fault at the roadside, then it's not covered.) It's a bargain compared to the more comprehensive rival services at £34.50 a year (£29.50 by direct debit). A roadside assistance service more comparable to the major rivals is £43 a year (£38 by direct debit).

Other Green Flag goodies include the usual pre-buy services for used cars (including an independent valuation), free route planning for members in the UK and Europe, and a range of European motoring services.

Britannia Rescue

Similar in its scope to Green Flag, Britannia has around 400,000 members. It too covers the car not the individual, although it's possible to extend to personal cover for an additional fee. It boasts the fastest average response time at 33 minutes; 95% of calls are attended within an hour. Priority is given to lone women and drivers with special needs.

Britannia's basic level of service includes roadside assistance, and recovery to a nearby garage. It costs a competitive £36.50 (£31.50 by direct debit). There's also a range of more comprehensive services.

Among Britannia's useful extras is a 24-hour free legal advice service, with representation if you're charged with a motoring offence. Cover also extends automatically to Eire, and there's optional European cover. There's also a facility to pay premiums monthly.

Guild of Experienced Motorists

Originally known as the Company of Veteran Motorists, the Guild of Experienced Motorists (GEM) retains a V-badge as its symbol. Membership is open only to drivers without any current endorsement for a serious driving offence.

GEM basic membership entitles you to a quarterly magazine and the usual range of free legal and technical advice, including free access to the HPI information service (see page 99). Without recovery services, it's £13.50 a year

(plus a £5 joining fee unless you pay by direct debit).

Recovery membership is individual-based and covers you in your own or a hired car. There's one class which includes a limited Home Start service, and in some circumstances overnight accommodation and alternative travel costs are covered. Roadside repairs handle all disasters including running out of petrol and flat tyres. At £41.50 for individual membership it's very competitively priced.

With GEM it's up to you to contact the garage of your choice and arrange recovery. You also make payment, which you claim back from GEM. Some will welcome the freedom of choice; others might prefer an organisation with tied agents.

Among other noteworthy services are mechanical breakdown insurance (for newer cars only) and a discount on Europ Assistance. (GEM does not provide its own European recovery service.) There's a driver assessment service too – see page 120.

Institute of Advanced Motorists

The IAM is focused around an advanced driving test, and membership is only open to drivers who pass the test. (More details of the test and associated services are on page 119.) There are local groups, a magazine three times a year, and a number of special deals available to IAM members.

RoSPA

RoSPA (The Royal Society for the Prevention of Accidents) isn't a breakdown-oriented organisation, but it is involved in motoring issues. Established over 80 years, it's involved in promoting safety, and thus helping to save lives and reducing injury, in a wide variety of contexts. Many of its members are corporate bodies but there is a category of individual Road Safety membership (current cost £35.25 inc. VAT). Of particular interest to those professionally involved with safety issues (although still of value to others), it provides access to RoSPA's advice and information service, and a subscription to their bimonthly Care on the Road journal.

The RoSPA Advanced Drivers' Association is open to those who pass the RoSPA Advanced Driving Test: more details are on page 119.

RoSPA also administers the National Safe Driving Awards Scheme, designed for drivers of company cars and other vehicles.

Would you buy the same colour again?	
An RAC survey found that not all drivers would! Re-buy ratings were:	
Red	94%
Silver	89%
Blue	86%
Black	80%
Other colours	71%
Grey	67%
Pastel (including lilac, beige and lime)	63%
Green	53%
White	44%

Driver
training

Learning to drive

Learner drivers in the UK can apply for a provisional driving licence after the age of 17 (16 for holders of mobility allowances). It's possible to drive on private land, but not on the public highway, when you're under 17. You must have your licence (and not simply have sent off for it) before you begin to drive.

It's not compulsory for you to be taught by an Approved Driving Instructor (ADI) but it is illegal to pay anyone to teach you unless they are either an ADI, or hold a Trainee Licence as a part-way step towards becoming an ADI.

Choosing a driving instructor

It's important to choose an instructor with whom you'll be happy learning. Ask friends and relatives who've learned to drive recently if they can recommend their instructor. Before settling on an instructor, check what they charge and what type of car you will learn on. It's helpful if you learn on a car as similar as possible to any car you'll be practising on between lessons. Dual controls (so the instructor can brake if necessary) give added reassurance, particularly when you're starting out.

The Driving Standards Agency (DSA) holds a register of ADIs

The ADIs are tested regularly and graded by the DSA. The grades go from 1 to 6 (with 6 as the highest) but even a grade one instructor will have gone through a rigorous testing programme. ADIs display green identification certificates (and trainees pink ones) on their windscreens.

You need to pass the theory test before you can apply to take the practical driving test. If you start learning with an ADI from the onset, they'll be able to give you advice on passing both tests.

Keep practising

Getting plenty of practice will increase your chances of learning quickly and passing your test. Learner drivers must be supervised by someone at least 21 years old who has held a full British licence for that type of car (automatic or manual) for at least three years.

The car must display L-plates (or D-plates in Wales) whenever a learner is in charge. The L-plates should be taken off or covered on private cars at all other times, although driving schools are allowed to leave them uncovered.

It's essential to ensure that the car you drive is properly insured. Ask the owner (or registered keeper) if it's insured for any driver; if not they will need to ask their insurer to add you as a named driver. Learners are not permitted to drive on motorways.

As well as getting on-the-road practice, it's important for learners to master the basics of driving theory and motoring regulations. The *Highway Code* should be every learner driver's bedtime reading; tackle it in short bursts. There are many other excellent books to help learners, including The Stationery Office's *The Driving Test* (which concentrates on the practical test), *The Official Theory Test for Car Drivers and Motorcyclists* (which lists the questions that are likely to be asked), and *The Driving Manual*, which deals particularly with practical driving skills.

The theory test

Both theory test and practical test can be taken at a large number of centres across the country. The theory test consists of 35 multiple-choice questions, covering aspects of driving theory and practice. It's necessary (at the time of writing) to get 30 questions right to pass the test.

The practical test

The standard practical driving test lasts about 35 minutes. There's a brief eyesight test, then the instructor accompanies the candidate as s/he drives along a varied route of normal roads, chosen to provide both a range of road and traffic conditions, and suitable locations for the set exercises that are included.

Set features of the test are an emergency stop and two out of three of exercises involving reversing round a corner, reverse parking and turning in the road.

The instructor will also be assessing how the candidate handles the controls and makes general progress. In order to pass it's necessary to show that you drive safely and confidently, reacting appropriately to traffic conditions, responding correctly to signals and handling manoeuvres safely and efficiently.

The standard driving test entitles you to drive 'Category B' vehicles – cars and some other small vehicles. In order to drive larger vehicles, or to tow a large trailer, it's necessary to take an additional test appropriate to the type of vehicle you want to drive.

In Galashiels 73.8% of test-takers passed the test in 1996/7, while in Wood Green, London, only 34.3% passed.

The extended test

Drivers who are retaking the test after being disqualified may be required to take an extended driving test. This lasts twice as long and is more demanding, covering a wider variety of roads usually including dual carriageways.

Not so lucky

In 1996/7, 1,386,404 car practical driving tests were taken. 44.7% of test-takers passed – a proportion which has been dropping steadily – so 628,041 people came home unhappy.

The top 5 reasons for car test failure, for 17-99 year olds inclusive, were:

Women:

1. Reversing Control

2. Ineffective Observation

3. Use of Steering

4. Reverse Park Under Control

5. Use of Gears

Men:

1. Ineffective Observation

2. Use of Steering

3. Reversing Control

4. Unduly Hesitant

5. Use of Gears

1,129,918 people took the car theory test in 1996/7. The pass level was raised (to 30 correct answers out of 35 questions) in October, and following that rise the pass level fell to 61.8%.

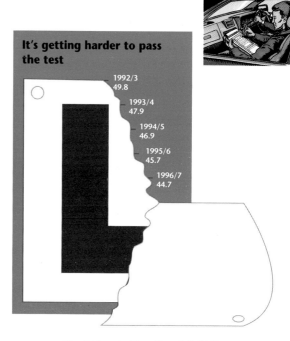

It's getting harder to pass the test

1992/3
49.8

1993/4
47.9

1994/5
46.9

1995/6
45.7

1996/7
44.7

Upgrading your skills

Passing the driving test shouldn't be the end of your learning as a motorist: it's only the start. To the experience that practice on the roads brings, you can add formal training in aspects of motoring not covered by the test, or advanced training in general driving techniques.

Obtaining an additional driving qualification will not only help you to drive more safely, it could also entitle you to cheaper insurance premiums.

As well as courses, there are a number of books and videos available for drivers working on improving their skills. The Stationery Office publishes *Roadcraft* and the *Roadcraft* video, which outline the Police method of safe driving, and the IAM and other organisations also offer advice and information.

Motorway driving

Since learners aren't allowed on motorways, you won't have any experience of motorway driving when you've just passed your test. Most ADIs offer motorway training, and it's worth having a lesson or two before you set off on that long motorway journey on your own.

Pass plus

Four good reasons why new drivers need extra training:

- One in five new drivers has an accident in their first year of driving.

- The risk of being injured or killed in a road accident is about six times greater for drivers aged 17-20 than for drivers aged 40 or over.

- Learner drivers are not allowed on motorways, so newly qualified drivers have no formal training in motorway driving.

- Insurers penalise new drivers because of their accident record – but reduce the penalties if they have extra training.

The Pass Plus scheme was launched in February 1995 by the DSA and the Department of Transport, and is supported by insurers representing over 60% of the UK private car market. It's open to drivers within a year of passing their practical driving test, and is designed to give them experience and confidence, and help improve road safety as result.

Pass Plus trainees take six lessons, covering attitudes and skills, night driving, all-weather driving, motorway driving, driving on dual carriageways and open roads.

There's no exam to take

Drivers who complete the course satisfactorily are given a certificate by their instructors, which entitles them to the equivalent of a one year's no claim discount on their insurance (from participating insurers). If you don't own a car but drive someone else's under their insurance, you can defer the concession for up to two years.

Full details are available from driving instructors, or by phoning 0115 955 7736.

Advanced driving tests

RoSPA Advanced Driving Test and Advanced Drivers' Association

The RoSPA Advanced Drivers' Association is open only to those who pass the RoSPA Advanced Driving Test. With over 10,000 members, it has a large number of local groups throughout the UK, which can offer free advice and assessments to those planning to take the test.

All RoSPA examiners hold a UK Police Class One driving qualification. The tests take at least 1¼ hours. Tests are graded Gold, Silver and Bronze (and 'Ungraded') and it's necessary for all ROAD members to take regular refresher tests.

Current cost of the test (including one year's ROAD membership) is £35; refresher tests are included in the lower continuing membership fees. Membership provides access to other group activities, and a subscription to the RoSPA magazine *Care on the Road*.

The Institute of Advanced Motorists Test

The IAM advanced driving test is a one hour test based on the principles of concentration, observation, anticipation and planning. It's open to those who passed their full driving test at least three months previously, and costs £27. The IAM's 300-plus examiners are all holders of the Police Advanced Driving Certificate, and agree with the taker a convenient location for the test.

Once you've passed the test, you're entitled to join the IAM, which has over 200 local groups. They publish a thrice-yearly magazine, *Advanced Driving*, and provide access to reduced insurance rates and other special offers.

If you'd like to check out your driving standard before plunging into the test, it's possible to obtain a free assessment from a volunteer observer in your local group. Associate Membership for those preparing to take the test is also available.

GEM Experienced Driver Assessment

The Guild of Experienced Motorists doesn't administer a formal test, but it does offer an assessment scheme, which is particularly useful for those who can't face a test but would still like an appraisal of their skills. Those busy Police Class One drivers help out again, offering advice during the one hour drive.

Refreshers, Skids and Circuits

You may want to undertake further training simply because you haven't driven for a while and need some reassurance before getting back on the road. Driving schools don't only teach learner drivers: most will gladly help old hands brush up their skills. Alternatively, ask your motoring organisation for advice; or SAGA (0800 300 500) run occasional Car Confidence Courses which are particularly helpful for older drivers.

Training in a skid pan is unbeatable for giving you experience at handling a skidding car. Again, your driving school or motoring organisation can point you to local resources. And if you fancy putting your foot down (legally) there are a number of racing circuits where you can go for training, or simply for enjoyment.

Useful addresses

The Association of British Insurers
51 Gresham Street
LONDON EC2V 7HQ
Tel. 0171 600 3333

The Automobile Association (AA)
Norfolk House
Priestley Road
BASINGSTOKE
Hants RG24 9NY
Tel. 0990 448866
To join: 0800 444 999
Emergency breakdown service:
0800 887766

Automobile Buyers Services Ltd
(specialist car inspection company)
Adelphi Mill
Grimshaw Lane
BOLLINGTON
Cheshire SK10 5JB
Tel. 01625 576441

Britannia Recovery Ltd
St George's Square
HUDDERSFIELD
West Yorkshire HD1 1JF
Tel. 01484 514848
To join: 0800 591 563

British Insurance Brokers Association
14 Bevis Marks
LONDON EC3A 7NT
Tel. 0171 623 9043

British Red Cross
9 Grosvenor Crescent
LONDON SW1X 7EJ
Tel. 0171 235 5454

The Caravan Club
East Grinstead House
EAST GRINSTEAD
W Sussex RH19 1UA
Tel. 01342 326944

Driver & Vehicle Licensing Agency (DVLA)
Driver & Vehicle Licensing Centre (DVLC)
SWANSEA SA99 1TU

For changes to your driving licence:
SWANSEA SA99 1BN
Driving licence enquiries:
Tel. 01792 772151
Car registration enquiries:
Tel. 01792 772134
Registration hotline (for custom number plates) – 0181 200 6565

Driving Instructors' Association (DIA)
Safety House
Beddington Farm Road
CROYDON CR0 4XZ
Tel. 0181 655 5151
Mail order (for list of member ADIs):
Tel. 0181 665 5253

Driving Standards Agency (DSA)
Stanley House
56 Talbot Street
NOTTINGHAM NG1 5GU
Tel. 0115 901 2500
Customer Service Unit:
Tel. 0115 901 2515/6

Environmental Transport Association
10 Church Street
WEYBRIDGE
Surrey KT13 8RS
Tel. 01932 828882

Finance and Leasing Association
(for credit and finance problems)
Imperial House
15-19 Kingsway
LONDON WC2B 6UN
Tel. 0171 836 6511

Green Flag
Green Flag House
Cote Lane
LEEDS LS28 5GF
Tel. 0113 236 3236
To join:
Green Flag
FREEPOST
Leeds LS99 3GF
or tel. 0800 001 301

Guild of Experienced Motorists (GEM)
Station Road
FOREST ROW
East Sussex RH18 5EN
Tel. 01342 825676

HPI Ltd (for information on used cars)
Dolphin House
P O Box 61
New Street
SALISBURY
Wilts SP1 2TB
Tel. 01722 422422

Institute of Advanced Motorists (IAM)
IAM House
359 Chiswick High Road
LONDON W4 4HS
Tel. 0181 994 4403

The Insurance Ombudsman Bureau
City Gate One
135 Park Street
LONDON SE1 9EA
Tel. 0171 928 7600

Mobility Advice and Vehicle Information Service (MAVIS)
(for disabled drivers)
Transport Research Laboratory
CROWTHORNE
Berks RG45 6AU
Tel. 01344 661000

Motor Insurers' Bureau
152 Silbury Boulevard
CENTRAL MILTON KEYNES
MK9 1NB
Tel. 01908 830001

Motor Schools Association of Great Britain Ltd
182A Heaton Moor Road
STOCKPORT
Cheshire SK4 4DU
Tel. 0161 443 1611

National Association of Approved Driving Instructors
90 Ash Lane
Halebarns
ALTRINCHAM
Cheshire WA15 8PB
Tel. 0161 980 5907

National Caravanning Council
Catherine House
Victoria Road
ALDERSHOT
Hants GU11 1SS
Tel. 01252 318251

National Trailer and Towing Association
Unit D, Great Fenton Business Park
Grove Road
Fenton
STOKE ON TRENT
Staffs ST4 4LZ
Tel. 01782 745646

The Royal Automobile Club (RAC)
14 Cockspur Street
LONDON SW1Y 5BL
Tel. 0171 389 8900

Commercial arm (and to join):
RAC Motoring Services Ltd
RAC House, M1 Cross
Brent Cross
LONDON NW2 1LT
Tel. 0800 029 029
Breakdown service: 0800 828 282

Retail Motor Industry Federation
9 North Street
RUGBY
CV21 2AB
Tel. 01788 576465

Royal Society for the Prevention of Accidents (RoSPA)
Edgbaston Park
353 Bristol Road
BIRMINGHAM B5 7ST
Tel. 0121248 2000

St Andrew's Ambulance Association
16 Torthichen Street
EDINBURGH EH3 8JB
Tel. 0131 229 5419

St John Ambulance Association and Brigade
1 Grosvenor Crescent
LONDON SW1X 7EF
Tel. 0171 251 0004
(for addresses of county headquarters, check your local phone book)

Society of Motor Auctions
P O Box 13
WILMSLOW PDO
Cheshire SK9 1LL
Tel. 01625 536937

Society of Motor Manufacturers and Traders (SMMT)
Forbes House
Halkin Street
LONDON SW1X 7DS
Tel. 0171 235 7000

Scottish Motor Trade Association
3 Palmerston Place
EDINBURGH EH12 5AQ
Tel. 0131 225 3643

Sold Secure (vehicle security)
Block 36, Northumbria Police Force HQ
Ponteland
Newcastle-upon-Tyne
NE20 0BL
Hotline: 0500 192 192

Vehicle Builders and Repairers Association
Belmont House
102 Finkle Lane
Gildersome
LEEDS LS27 7TW
Tel. 0113 253 8333

Vehicle Inspectorate
Berkeley House
Croydon Street
BRISTOL BS5 0DA
Tel. 0117 954 3200

Metric/Imperial Conversions

Kilometres – Miles

km	miles or km	miles
1.61	1	0.62
3.22	2	1.24
4.83	3	1.86
6.44	4	2.49
8.05	5	3.11
9.66	6	3.73
11.27	7	4.35
12.87	8	4.97
14.48	9	5.59
16.09	10	6.21
32.19	20	12.43
48.28	30	18.64
64.37	40	24.86
80.47	50	31.07
96.56	60	37.28
112.63	70	43.47
160.93	100	62.14
321.87	200	124.27
804.67	500	310.69

Litres – Gallons

Litres	gallons or litres	Gallons
4.55	1	0.22
9.09	2	0.44
13.64	3	0.66
18.18	4	0.88
22.73	5	1.10
27.28	6	1.32
31.82	7	1.54
36.37	8	1.76
40.91	9	1.98
45.46	10	2.20
90.92	20	4.40
136.38	30	6.60
181.84	40	8.80
227.30	50	11.00
454.60	100	22.00

Tyre pressure

lb/sq. in (psi)	kg/sq cm
10	0.70
15	1.06
20	1.41
22	1.55
24	1.69
26	1.83
28	1.97
30	2.11
32	2.25
34	2.39

Index